Business Planning for Small Business

A step-by-step guide to the what, why, when and how of business planning

D R . W A R R E N H A R M E R

BALBOA.
PRESS

A DIVISION OF HAY HOUSE

Balboa Press books may be ordered through booksellers or by contacting:

Balboa Press
A Division of Hay House
1663 Liberty Drive
Bloomington, IN 47403
www.balboapress.com.au
1 (877) 407-4847

Because of the dynamic nature of the Internet, any web addresses or
links contained in this book may have changed since publication and may
no longer be valid. The views expressed in this work are solely those
of the author and do not necessarily reflect the views of the publisher,
and the publisher hereby disclaims any responsibility for them.

The author of this book does not dispense medical advice or prescribe the use
of any technique as a form of treatment for physical, emotional, or medical
problems without the advice of a physician, either directly or indirectly. The
intent of the author is only to offer information of a general nature to help
you in your quest for emotional and spiritual well-being. In the event you use
any of the information in this book for yourself, which is your constitutional
right, the author and the publisher assume no responsibility for your actions.

Any people depicted in stock imagery provided by Thinkstock are models,
and such images are being used for illustrative purposes only.
Certain stock imagery © Thinkstock.

Printed in the United States of America.

ISBN: 978-1-4525-2684-3 (sc)
ISBN: 978-1-4525-2685-0 (e)

Balboa Press rev. date: 12/12/2014

Contents

PART 1

All about Business Planning

Introduction

Business consulting is an interesting profession and one that has given me permission to look where others aren't allowed. Small-business owners are extremely private about what goes on behind the counter, but my clients have let me poke, prod, peer, and dissect their businesses. They have laid it all bare: the good and the bad, the management triumphs, failings, and incompetencies. It's like the business edition of *Embarrassing Bodies*.

As a consultant, one of the first questions you ever ask your clients is, "Do you have a business plan?" The response is rarely positive. From the hundreds of businesses I have worked with, I estimate 5 percent have ever had business plans of any description. Of those, most were created because a bank asked for it as part of a loan application, then it was shelved and never looked at again. Even fewer businesses use planning as an ongoing practice; my guess is about 1 percent. These are sobering numbers, especially when we so frequently hear about the struggles of small business and the reported numbers of business failures.

Since planning practices are so rare in small business, you might expect there must be some difficult and onerous obstacles. After all, owning a business is probably the most financially risky thing anyone will ever do. Strangely, this level of risk doesn't seem to be widely understood, and due diligence for this is often much lower than it is for other types of investments, such as property or shares. A common response is, "My business plan is in my head." As part of countless business planning projects, I have taken all the information in the business owner's head and put it on paper. Not surprisingly, there were a many unanswered questions, no detailed financial projections, risk assessments, or marketing plans in those heads.

Even if you read this book cover to cover, most of you still won't do any kind of business planning. I have wondered why so few business owners never commit to the process, even when the benefits are comprehensive. Here are the main reasons I have seen and heard.

No need. The business is doing okay without it, so what's the point?

Overconfidence/ignorance (especially for new businesses). "I'm smart; how hard can it be?"

No capacity. Operating the business is challenging enough, and doing anything on top of that is beyond the owner's capability.

Don't know how. Having never done it before or not knowing what's involved, it all seems too hard.

Too expensive. Those who don't feel confident enough to do it themselves see the cost of getting professional help as too high and have the perception of no return.

No time. Too busy running the business.

Not implemented. Even if some kind of business planning is done, the actions and milestones are not followed

Only done once. The original business plan has never been updated.

Having seen hundreds of small businesses whose owners never did any business planning, I can say with confidence these are all excuses. If you want a well-run, professional, growing business, you have a greater chance of success if you are disciplined in planning your business.

You can overcome all of these small challenges, but to make this work you will need

- discipline to develop the planning habit (ongoing, not just once);
- a change of attitude and shift in priorities; and
- to make time—not a lot, but it needs to be dedicated.

People are people. Some are motivated and organised, while others cruise along. We all know which ones are more likely to succeed; it's up to you to decide if you can be bothered. What I can say with certainty is that business owners love having plans created for them, followed by someone making them stick to it. Having an experienced business consultant to help makes a very big difference.

About This Book

I have a number of objectives for this book.

1. Guidebook

For those who want or need to start business planning, this book shows you how to do it.

2. Explain value

In this book I aim to change your mind, to compel you to step away from your daily grind and take a bird's-eye view not just of your business but of your market and business landscape. Get out of your business for a short time and stop driving it in circles. Decide where exactly you want to go and how you will get there.

3. Demystify

For you to do business planning, it needs to be easy, simple, and accessible. I educate you and debunk any feelings of complexity or mystery about business planning you have.

How to Use This Book

You bought this book because you want to know more about business planning, but each of your needs will be different. Some will be in a hurry, because they urgently need to create a business plan to get a loan, a licence, an investor, or for a similar purpose. Others want to take more time or already have a business and want incorporate business planning into it. There are those who want to start a business and need to find answers to many questions before they get started.

This book has two parts, with chapters suited to different business planning needs, so you don't need to read every chapter. Part 1 contains background information about business planning particular to different stages of business and situations. Part 2 is a how-to section that gives detailed information, instruction, and examples of how to create business plans. Refer to the chapters as you create your plan to guide you through the process.

Here's a road map for deciding which sections to read.

Your situation	Why you want a business plan	Chapters to read first	Then
New business	To prepare yourself for business ownership and manage risk	1, 2, 5	Part 2
New business	For bank, finance, investor, accreditation, or other organisation	1, 4, 5	Part 2
Operating business	For a bank, finance, investor, accreditation, or other organisation	1, 4, 5	Part 2
Operating business	To review and take stock of your business, and to research and determine your future.	1, 3, 5	Part 2

Business Plans, from the Beginning

1

The future is not certain for anyone, but when you are business owner, that uncertainty feels starker. On any day, things can happen that can have a big impact on you: loss of clients, equipment failures, a tax bill, or the departure of a key staff member. Despite this, everyone who owns a business (or wants to) dreams about its future. When I speak to business owners about their business goals, they dream of earning more money, working less, and spending more time managing rather than running their businesses. Feeling *successful*, in all its forms, is a common desire. Those who are more ambitious plan for nationwide expansion, million-dollar profits, and market dominance. The less ambitious look for lifestyle.

By its nature, ambition amongst business owners means there is always a grander plan than just going to work the next day. To me that means business planning is already happening in every business, even in its crudest, loosest form. When I press business owners to tell me their goals for the next year, they can always come up with five to ten goals, as I am sure you could too. Dreams are not useful for creating action and maintaining the discipline needed to turn them into reality, which is why business planning is so powerful. In the process of planning you create a record and road map you can follow to reach those dreams.

What Is a Business Plan?

The term "business plan" can encompass many types that differ in format, layout, content, and purpose. Business gurus love to claim their own types as being the *definitive* plan and spruik their own methods to create them and their value to your business. There are countless books, articles, and how-tos on the subject, each with their own angles and glory for the authors. It is not useful or honest to say there is only one type. In my opinion, it is better to do some type of planning rather than getting hung up on differences in methods. I liken it to keeping fit. You are better off doing some exercise rather than none and can start getting picky once you get proficient.

After seeing what is needed in practice for small business, my definition of a business plan is:

A document that specifies and explains the goals of a business for a defined time period.

Sounds basic, so I will unpack it to explain my thinking.

- This definition is not too prescriptive, since the methods that work will differ between industries, businesses, markets, personalities, and the life stage of your business.
- To document means it is recorded in some way that is sharable and not just talk or thoughts. Since there are so many types of business plans, I do not think it is accurate or helpful to give more details about content, length, style, and so on. It could be one page, it could be all on a spreadsheet, hard or soft copy or it could be a designed and printed book.
- The plan gives definite, clear, measurable, and specific goals for the business; it specifies. That can include any number of metrics for the business, including, financials,

sales targets, budgets, marketing numbers, staff, retention, or sales ratios. It may also include other goals, such as moving to new premises, buying equipment, gaining accreditation, or winning an award.

- That it "explains" means all the necessary details are included to justify, back up, and convince the reader goals are achievable and based on solid reasoning and accurate information. Under this banner falls market research, competitor research, analyses, explanations, rationales, details, actions, timelines, milestones, theories, and risks.

- A "defined time period" is the plan's time frame, usually one to three years. The longer the time frame, the more granular details become.

Planning Practices

"Business planning" is a term I prefer to use rather than "business plan." Business planning is not a one-off activity, nor something you should do when you start your business, or when you feel motivated, and then forget about it. It is an ongoing process of development and review, of looking backwards and then looking forwards. With my clients I like to talk about planning practices. This is the day-to-day, week-to-week type of business planning that you actually use when you run your business. It is not just the creation of a document. Rather, the document is a summary of your planning. This is the discipline of developing habits and thinking strategically, the "working on the business" we always hear about but never seems to happen.

In your planning you will research your market, create budgets and projections, plan your marketing, create an action plan, set milestones, review your business, and set goals. In most situations, these are all recorded in a single document, your business plan. If you are doing this process to have a better business, it's less important what type of plan you use than it is to be doing it.

Business Planning Process

There is a common sequence of events involved in business planning regardless of which type of business plan you create or methodology you follow. How this process works in reality depends on your purpose, your business, whether your business is new or existing, and for whom the final plan will be prepared. For each type, the duration and emphasis of each stage will differ, as will the final product. More details about the variations is given in each of the business plan sections (chapters 2–4).

---

1. Decide to start business planning/write a business plan.
It sounds obvious, but the planning takes commitment, so having a clear point of decision defines the start of your commitment. In many cases this will be mandatory (for example, for a business finance application).

---

2. Determine scope and method.
Your final document could be a spreadsheet, a hundred-page document, or anything in between, with many possible degrees of detail. Decide what you are going to do before you start. If you are creating a business plan for a specific purpose, the scope will be largely predetermined. In this step you decide which template to start with.

---

3. Research.
As you gather information, you add this into your template to start creating your plan.

---

4. Document.
Once the raw data is entered, you refine, shape, and edit it to create clear communication of your plans, research, goals, projections, and actions. Step 3 and 4 are often done back and forth. As you add research results, review and determine what further information is needed.

> 5. Sanity check
> Once your plan is at draft stage, getting an independent expert to review is needed to ensure the plan is reasonable and realistic. Once you have this feedback, you will most likely go back to step 3 or 4 to fine-tune your plan.

> 6. Submit/implement.
> With the completed plan, you will take definite actions and create an ongoing review program. If you have created a business plan for approval or application, it will be submitted.

Types of Plans

There are many types of business plans, including one-page business plans, compliance plans, and business plans for bank financing. You will find countless examples on the Internet, each focusing on particular content or methods, varying with the purpose of the plan or who is selling your their vision (or services). All plans are essentially variations on the same theme, and you will find most templates have pretty much the same sections (give or take), with titles and emphases differing. For example, a business plan aiming to secure financing will have a short, clear vision of the business, thorough and solid financials, and show the reader you are well prepared and know your stuff. On the other hand, business plans used to gain licences will have a heavy emphasis on meeting compliance requirements particular to that organisation.

From the business plans I have seen and worked on, I tend to categorise them into two types that divide them by purpose, hence define the way you go about creating them. I use these definitions extensively throughout this book and base my guides to business plan preparation around them.

Plans for Yourself

This type of planning is a slower, more introspective process of review, strategy, direction, and action. It is ongoing and part of your regular business activities, where you will periodically review your business, map your future, and determine actions and milestones. It is a process that you undertake to plan, research, learn, strategize, discover, ask questions, identify risks, and work out how you will make your business work. Your final business plan simply documents everything you discover and all of decisions you make. The point of this type of business planning is not to create a perfect document.

This type of planning is often more involved and takes longer, but the final product is more variable. I have seen business plans that are spreadsheets or individual documents not collated into a single document, which work just fine for those businesses. You just need to use it for the true purpose: to improve your business. You will find more about this type of business planning in chapter 2 (for new businesses) and chapter 3 (for operating businesses).

Business Plans for Others

As you move through your business journey, it is not uncommon to be required to submit a business plan to gain approval for a particular business application. For example,

- Applying for loans or other types of financing
- Applying for particular business licences, such as a builder's licence or to become a Registered Training Organisation (RTO)
- Pitching to investors

- Business migration visas
- Part of a course of study

These types of business plans generally have defined requirements about format, content, and structure. For the best chances at acceptance, they need to be shorter, very concise, and clearly meet the prescribed criteria. In this case, it's is all about the document, which needs to be as professional and perfect as possible. The process is often much tighter due to deadlines, and you may spend less time thinking and discussing during the planning process.

Even though the emphasis of these plans is different than plans you create for yourself, you can still extract some of the true value of business planning, as you still conduct research and create a road map for your business future, even though it is usually less comprehensive.

What Does a Business Plan Look Like?

Before you start creating your own plan, take some time to scan a few different types of business plans to get a feel for the way they look and what is in them. You will find a number of examples at www.businessplancompany.com.au, as well as many others sites on the Internet.

Following is a list of sections commonly found in business plans, with some comments on each and when they might have more or less emphasis. Exact formats, section sequences, and titles vary slightly. For example, you may have a section on growth that includes targets, strategy, and marketing. In another plan, marketing may be a section on its own. In this book I have endeavoured to make the section names as generic as possible, so you can easily fit them into your template.

Executive Summary	1-2 page summary of the contents of the business plan
Introduction	All information about you, company details, addresses, date, contact details, business registration details and so on
Business Description, Concept, Products, and Services	A concise and clear description of your business overview, concept, products and services, vision, mission, and values
S.W.O.T.	Analysis of strengths, weaknesses, opportunities, and threats
Legal/Regulation/ Insurance/Compliance	Details of insurances, licences, and any other relevant information
Location/Venue/Facility	Description of the place you will do business, manufacture, sell, or store your products or services
History	An overview of the business' history
The Market	An analysis of your target market, your target customers, how many customers there are, industry trends, competitors, interpretation of where you sit, and what makes you different
Business Goals/Growth Targets	Plans for business growth, goals, and strategy
Marketing	A description of marketing you will undertake, marketing materials, costs, and how you will measure your results
Sales	How you will sell your products and/or services
Operations	Overview of key elements in your business operation
Equipment and Infrastructure	Description of tools, equipment, premises, IT, and other requirements, both current and future

People	Details of your team; what roles members will take, position descriptions; organisational chart; how many are on the team; and how you will recruit, retain, and manage your current and future team members
Risks	Risks and how you will minimise them
Sourcing, Procurement, Inventory, and Logistics	Description of the purchasing, storage, and movement of goods in your business
Timeline	A time-based analysis of key projects or business start-up
Website and Internet	A description of your website and online requirements
IT	A description of IT requirements
Financials-Projections, Cash Flow and Balance Sheet, Break Even	Detailed projected financial statements for the next one to three years
Financial Start-Up Costs/ Project Costs	Detailed financial analysis of project costs or start-up costs
Action Plan	A detailed list of upcoming projects with timelines
Appendix / References / Additional information	List of all references used in the plan and any detailed supplementary information.

Templates Explained

Starting with a prepopulated business plan template is standard practice, even for professional business planners. Templates are a document with all of the section headings of your plan already prepared. You insert all the details relevant to your business into the document. There are many available, with essentially the same sections, although the sequence or section titles may differ. The following is an example of a typical page from a template below.

5. The Market.

5.1 Overview

5.2 Current products and services

5.3 Target markets

Market 1

Description
•
Needs
•
Messages
•
Actions
•

5.4 Market needs

5.5 Competition

5.6 Value proposition

5.7 Market size

5.8 Industry trends

5.9 Technology

Some templates go further than just headings and contain content-specific information, usually tailored for a particular business type (e.g., plumbing). You can enter your own details, but the content is generic cut-and-paste. Avoid these if you are want business planning to be a valuable part of your business practice. You need to think, talk, and research, not just add in names. This practice is akin to photocopying a book and expecting to learn something in the process.

Whilst templates are the starting point for any business plan, as you fill in the content, the headings and emphasis may change, depending on your situation and business. For this reason, don't get too hung up on which template is "best" unless it has been prescribed as part of an application. Just start with one, and let it evolve. You will expand sections that need more detail, whilst others that are less relevant may just be simple statements or left out altogether. For example, I worked on a plan for a new type of medical business where the service needed in-depth description, so I added a separate section. In businesses where there is no staff, those sections are left out.

Many business *Plans for Others* have specific, mandated criteria or templates. Before you set off on creating your plan, check whether this is the case for you application. Understanding not only what template is required but also what information is vital for your application to be successful.

Sanity Check

In reality, you can put whatever you like in your business plan—meteoric growth projections, rapid rise to wealth, high profit margins, and no loss of clients. However, creating an overwhelmingly successful picture of your future business with no challenges is not realistic, nor useful. If the business plan is for someone other than you (like a bank), your credibility will evaporate as soon as they read it, and your application is less likely to be approved. If the plan is for your own strategy/management purposes, it will become irrelevant as soon as your actual results start to deviate from the planned results, and you won't use it as a reference anymore. Further, you will be ill-prepared for the inevitable ups and downs of business ownership, which defeats the purpose of business planning in the first place.

If you haven't been in business before, it can be difficult to create a plan that is realistic or thorough enough, because you don't have the experience or knowledge to ask the right questions or know what is realistic. Business planning is a process of opening your eyes. In this process, you must accept that there are many things you don't know you that you don't know.

For this reason, getting external advice or input is essential, at the very least to check your plan once the draft is complete to assure it is reasonable. The aim is to make your plan as realistic as possible, so challenging your assumptions is very important to make sure they are robust and will stand up to the rigour of the real business world. The ideal situation is to have an experienced small-business consultant work with you to guide you through the whole process. But business owners—especially new business owners—are often terrified of the costs of professional advice. Remember, good, solid advice from an experienced consultant is a wise investment that can save you thousands later on.

For those on a super-low budget, you may find government-sponsored business mentors who can give you guidance or have friends and family experienced in small business who you can ask. An experienced businessperson can look at your plan, ask questions, and add considerable value.

How accurate your business plan will be comes down to how well you research. If you have the time, persistence, and resources, you can create a good road map that helps you to truly understand the reality of owning a business.

2

Business Planning for New Businesses

In this chapter I talk about business planning for new business owners that intend to create a *Plan for Yourself* and want to really understand your new business before you start. This is a slower process of researching a new business in a comprehensive way that will lead to more-competent business management and a more in-depth understanding of how your business will operate. On top of the refinement of your business strategy, you will undergo a personal transformation that will make you a more-informed and better-prepared business owner.

If you want to create a business plan solely for the purpose of investors, financiers, loans, banks, licences, or any other approvals, go straight to chapter 4.

The Reality of Owning Your Own Business

Starting a business is a big undertaking. It's a bold, courageous move that is very exciting, but it does carry risk, a lot more risk than most new business owners realise. When I started my first business (a restaurant), I was not long out of university, overconfident, and totally ignorant. I remember flippantly commenting to a work colleague, "How hard can it be?" Now, after many years in business, I know that small business presents a unique set of challenges. To succeed you need to be a multiskilled person who can juggle many issues, priorities, and diverse responsibilities at the same time.

Most of you who start a new business will do so like I did: with brazen optimism, taking the leap into business bursting with enthusiasm and energy, oblivious to the risks that lie ahead. In doing so, you won't adequately prepare. Many businesses start but don't make it; it is much easier to be one of the casualties than one of the successes. It is easy to be dazzled by stories of amazingly successful businesses that started in their garage, but they are exceptionally rare. Hard work does not mean success in small business, but cleverness and persistence do.

Why Bother with Business Planning?

Planning Your Journey

Imagine you are about to set off on a very long journey in your car, across an unknown landscape to a distant destination you have never visited before. You aren't sure when you will return (if ever), you don't have a map, there are no road signs, and you only have limited information about the destination. Would you just get in your car and drive? Or would you first plan your journey, map out your route, check on fuel locations, get your car serviced, and research your destination? Starting a business really is starting a journey into the unknown. Despite all wishful thinking, you don't really know for sure how it will turn out, and unfortunately, the statistics are against your venture being a raging success.

Starting a small business with no business planning is the equivalent of making a journey with no road map. It is possible you will have a safe, uneventful journey, followed by seamlessly settling in when you arrive. However, it's more likely that you will get lost, find unexpected forks in the road, follow wrong signs, and have breakdowns. All these upsets will cost you money (from limited funds), waste time, and cause many headaches. I have heard hundreds of such horror stories and can say with certainty that some will happen to you.

For new businesses, business planning is about creating the most accurate picture of business *before* you start. It's like creating a travel plan and road map for your long journey, so you increase the chances of getting there safely and being happy when you get there. The more detail, information, and knowledge you have, the greater your chances of avoiding traps and minimising their impact when they do come along. Your business plan is also your chance to dream and to draw your picture of what your business will look like in future. It is a process of clarifying where you want your business to go and of reviewing and creating strategies to take you there. It is about creating a plan and then renewing your focus on the long term. By going through this process, you become equipped to make split-second decisions in line with your long-term goals. You will find yourself asking, "Is this in line with our overall plan and strategy?" because you actually know what your strategy is.

Your Juggling Skills

One of the biggest challenges of owning a small business is the number of business functions you need to manage at once. You will need to make decisions on a staggering range of issues, which could include anything from hiring staff, deciding where you will spend your marketing, managing cash flow, getting your clients to pay you, and maintaining IT systems—all in the same day.

In your planning process, you determine how these functions operate, so you will be better equipped to make more effective decision on the fly. When faced with a crossroad on your business journey, you can go back to the road map, reorient yourself, and feel more confident that you are going in the right direction. One of my engineering clients experienced extreme stress for a six-month period as the market for engineers dried up. This became very tough for all the team, who became overworked. Communication became reactive, and morale dropped. Through a regular sharing and discussing of the business plan, the team stayed focused in the right direction and acted cohesively to stay on track.

Make Your Mistakes on Paper

As you run your business, you will have to make a lot of decisions. Some of them are small, operational ones that just keep your business going. But there are some bigger, important decisions that involve spending money, often large sums. Such decisions could be choosing stock for the next season in your retail store, deciding whether to get a new website, hiring a new staff member, or doing an advertising campaign. Making the best decisions to take your business in the right direction is not always easy, with most small businesses using a trial-and-error approach. They try random approaches each time, making decisions on the spot and hoping the new approach will work better than the last. I have seen businesses spend $8,000 on a radio advertising campaign with no sales, hiring the wrong staff members, which wasted $25,000, and moving premises that resulted in a loss of trade (total cost $70,000).

A crystal ball would be very helpful when you are faced with big decisions, so you can act with certainty. Business planning enables you to draw out your options, research, and get a more realistic idea of how things might work out rather than flying blind. It is a process of opening your eyes, minimising risk, and maximising chances of success.

What Business Planning Does

For a new business, business planning,

- Creates a detailed, clear vision of your business based on your business ideas and goals
- Creates a list of tasks you need to undertake
- Sets milestones
- Creates a road map to keep you focused
- Improves decision making, especially day-to-day decision making, to keep you focused on long-term goals
- Makes a virtual assessment of your business idea before you decide to start
- Draws a financial picture of your business so you understand start-up costs, operating costs, pricing, and sales targets
- Forces you to make decisions on details that will have a big impact on your business
- Determines viability/feasibility

The Business Planning Process—New Businesses

The business planning process is given in the following table. Emphases is given on each component of the process as it applies to new businesses.

1. Decision to start business planning/write a business plan	
2. Determine scope and method, select a template	Since you are new to business, you may take more time to explore options before you get started.
3. Research	This is the most important part of process for new businesses, so it will take time.

4. Document	For new businesses, it is best to stick to an established template.
5. Sanity check	Very important. Your business concept and proposal need rigorous checking. There may be many cycles of research-documentation-sanity check before the process is complete.
6. Submit/Implement	Crucial. Your actions and plan will be referred to regularly as you proceed to start-up phase.

Total preparation time is fifteen to thirty hours. To do a thorough job researching and planning for a new business, I expect the process to take four to eight weeks, depending on how complex your business is and how deep into the research you go.

Typical length is twenty to thirty pages plus detailed financials. Since every business is different, length varies enormously. During your sanity check, you can gauge whether you need more or less detail.

Templates, style, and format should be standard, since you are new to business. Create a formal document, even if it is not completely polished to presentation standard. Once your business is in operation and you are making revisions and updates to your planning, content can be collated in forms that are less strict, but the discipline of putting the document together is very useful at this early stage. Your presentation style needs to be easily understood and followed by you and others in your business, so include the appropriate level of detail.

After Your Plan Is Finished

To Start or not to Start?

Once you have completed your business plan and have a better idea of what your business will look like and what is involved to start it, you may not like what you see. This is not unusual and, in fact, is part of the purpose. If you decide not to proceed with your business in that format at that time, that is an equally good outcome. You can then reassess the business you are proposing, perhaps delay the start, source more investment, find a business partner, or perhaps not start a business at all. The business plan would have achieved its purpose of making you better informed of your options and maybe saved you a lot of money and stress. When you make your final decision to start, consider the opportunity cost.

One of my business-planning clients was a middle-aged couple who intended to start an art gallery and cafe. They were ready to pay a deposit on a property that would involve a substantial financial commitment that would last many years. Before they started, we created a business plan for their proposal. We researched every aspect of their proposed business, including financial viability, council permits, traffic patterns, marketing, and the demands of running the business. In the end, the couple decided to start a much simpler, less-demanding, and lower-risk online business.

Following Your Road Map

Opening the doors to start trading does not mean the end of your business planning. You will move from theory mode to operation mode and will start to see how the business works in comparison to your plan. For your plan to become a useful document, it must become a guide that you refer to as you run your business. It is important that smaller actions and tasks are taken from the plan and transferred into your weekly and monthly activities.

Refer back to it, and measure your progress against the targets and strategies described. The most valuable thing you can take from your planning is a change in attitude. Planning is an ongoing process that never ends as long as you are in business.

Even larger organisations are not always good at implementation. I once did some strategy work for a government body. A senior member of the project team said to me, "We have a bookshelf full of strategy plans that have never been implemented."

Bringing Your Plan to Life

What follows is a typical business review and planning schedule. Set aside regular time (monthly and weekly) to take a bird's-eye view of the business. Look at how your plans are working out, developing key measures that will tell you whether you are on track. When your business is not doing what you planned, take time to find out what is happening and really understand how your business and market operate. This ongoing process of learning is vital to continued growth and survival. It is a good idea to create your own "board" of interested and experienced people who can review your progress with you.

Time or Event	What to Do
New business, change in direction or market/ business conditions	• Create a new comprehensive business plan. • Explore current issues or changes in depth. • Create action plan and recommendations.
Annually	• Review your business plan to see how the year went, in comparison to the plan. Try to understand the reasons your business performed differently from your expectations. • Create a new plan for the upcoming year. • Determine your major projects for the year, including milestones. • Set actions and tasks to achieve objectives. • Define marketing activities, budgets, and initiatives.

Monthly	• Review monthly results compared to your plan and budget. • Host a monthly "board" review meeting. • Review tasks and actions from your business plan. • Implement actions. • Review new developments.
Daily, weekly	• Review weekly results. • Review actions from business plan. • Ensure tasks, actions, and systems are being implemented. • Ensure all activities are being measured. • Refresh your memory about the bigger picture; measure your weekly results compared to the annual plan.

Taking words off a page and turning them into actions, accountabilities, and milestones is not too difficult to do, but it does take some discipline and forward planning. Here's how to do it.

Budgets, Projections, Sales, and Other Metrics

From your projections you can take your monthly sales, costs, and profit targets and track them against actual figures each month. If you have not created sales targets within your projections, it is a good idea to do so. At your monthly board/review meeting, present analyses of business performance against your plan. Discuss variations from the plan and reasons for them. If you do not have a timeline and marketing schedule/budget, they are very useful.

Actions

As you go through your planning process, create a list of projects and actions you need to undertake as identified in your plan. Create a master list of these and then a timeline, so you can review your progress during the year.

1. For each section of your plan, identify actions that you need to take.

Examples

Action	
Create Facebook page	High

Action	
Job Descriptions—update	Medium

Action	
Review website	Low

2. At the end of your plan, summarise your actions, and rank them in monthly priorities with the person responsible.

Examples

July	
Create Facebook page	David
Hire new salesperson	Maria
Start new accounting system	Warren
New marketing campaign—local schools	Warren

3. Add actions to your calendar and/or to-do lists each month, so they become part of your daily routine; include deadlines.
4. At your monthly review meeting, report on the progress of each project.

Your Plan vs. Reality

You can put whatever you like in your business plan: fast growth, great profits, and new markets; the sky is the limit. But once your business is operating and you start tracking your results against your plan, your assumptions will be tested, and you will see how accurate they are. Business planning is great for setting targets and stretching goals, but if your goals are unrealistic, your plan will become irrelevant very quickly, and you will stop using it. It's fair to say that business plans for the most part assume that your business outlook is rosier and more easily achieved than usually happens.

Some typical examples that I have seen include,

- Growth targets are not realistic.
- Sales targets are too high.
- Profit margins are too high.
- Costs are forgotten or too low.
- Assumptions about the market not accurate.
- Sales processes and times not well understood.
- Understanding of financial measures is lacking.
- Ability to achieve goals is overestimated.

Getting your assumptions right for new businesses is tricky, since you have no trading history to guide you. This places a great deal of importance on the sanity check. Experienced consultants and businesspeople can tell you quickly if your proposed results are reasonable. If they come back with feedback that it is not, you will need to go back and review your assumptions. When creating a business plan with a new media company, the business owner had made assumptions about corporate sales with large sale prices. In reality, this sector of the market was very difficult to crack, but small businesses were much more enthusiastic, so we had to revisit the plan to adjust.

If your assumptions are way off, it's a good idea to revisit your plan quickly and revise your targets based on the updated information. Business planning is a process of reiteration; the best data you can get that will predict your future comes from your own business. By analysing all the detailed metrics in your business, you will be able to know what is reasonable and can then strategize how to achieve your targets. A health services client had two main service streams, and growth was predicted to be equal in both streams. What actually happened was that demand for stream 2 grew suddenly due to change in regulation, whilst stream 1 grew more slowly. Monthly financial reviews of budget vs. actual revenue quickly picked up the trend, so greater focus was placed in stream 2 for management and also new business development.

For more information on writing a business plan, go to part 2.

3

Business Planning for Operating Businesses

In this chapter I talk about business *Plans for Yourself*, for operating businesses, that is, those who intend to create a business plan in order to review their businesses. This is the most in-depth type of business planning. It is a slower, more comprehensive process that delves deeper into your business, creates a deeper understanding of how your business and market operate, and creates goals and a road map for the future. There are many methods for this type of planning, too many for a single book. The methods I describe later in this book favour a more traditional style of business planning, but the reasons behind it and ongoing planning are equally true, regardless of which method you choose.

If you want to create a business plan solely for the purpose of investors, financiers, loans, banks, licences or any other approvals, go to Chapter 4.

Why Bother with Business Planning?

Since you are in business already, you already know firsthand the challenges of owning a business and how difficult it can be to step away in order to make objective decisions. Dealing with day-to-day operations and spot fires can be all too consuming, with weeks and months passing without working on longer-term strategic projects. The business planning process is all about taking the time to stop, taking a bird's-eye view, determining where you want to go, and ensuring you are actually going there.

Business planning

- Creates a detailed, clear vision of your business future
- Creates a list of actions, tasks, and milestones you can measure your performance against
- Improves decision making—especially day-to-day decision making—to keep you focused on long-term goals
- Makes a virtual assessment of business ideas and directions before you commit to them
- Forces you to make decisions
- Creates a new budget
- Challenges your assumptions about the business
- Reviews your business operations
- Updates knowledge of your market

The Parts You Need to Do

Every business has its own practices and routines, each done with different levels of detail and diligence. The least organised businesses have never done any business planning or reviews, while the most organised have structured, regular reviews and monthly board meetings. Where you sit in this spectrum dictates what you need to do to start business planning.

The following table contains an overview of types of business planning practices for operating businesses. Because operating businesses with business plans don't need to update all parts of the plan every year, you may update different sections of the plan at different intervals. It is okay to pick and choose business plan components as per the schedule, but you should plan to do a business review every few years. If you have never done one, it is essential you do a full plan, otherwise, you will miss out on important, small details that can help you build a better business.

What you need to do ...	if
Create a full business plan.	• You have never done one before. • Your market has changed. • You are making a big decision about your business. • You are contemplating a big change, new market, or new product.
Set business goals, actions, and milestones.	• At least annually; if your business is growing fast, update biannually.
Budgets and projections	• Update at least annually.
Market analysis	• You have never done it before. • You are introducing a new product or service. • Your marketing is not working. • You are getting intelligence that the market is changing. • New competitors are appearing that you don't know about. • Pricing has become more of an issue with your clients. • You are losing clients.
Marketing plan	• Update at least annually.
Operation plan	• You have never done it before. • You are introducing a new product or service. • Your current operations are not working effectively.

Business Planning Process—Operating Businesses

The business planning process is shown in the following table, explaining the emphases on each component of the process as it applies to operating businesses.

	Already Business Planning	No Business Planning
1. Decide to start business planning/ write a business plan.	You will already have a planning and review schedule for your business, so this stage is simply following the plan.	Start now.
2. Determine scope and method, select a template.	If you have planning practices in place, you may follow your previous practices or review them and make changes as necessary.	This is an important step to make sure you are committed to the process. Take time to plan and understand what you need to do.
3. Research	Depending on how recently you completed your last plan, the level of time and detail will vary.	Your business and market needs thorough review and research, so this will take longer.
4. Document	Shorter and more flexible. Since this is internal document, it needs to be in a format you will use and refer to.	
5. Sanity check	Since you already know how your business operates, many of your assumptions have been tested. Getting external advice is valuable to make sure your plan is realistic, especially if you are planning new products, big decisions, or new markets.	
6. Implement	Crucial. Your actions and plan will be referred to regularly as operate your business.	

Total preparation time is ten to thirty hours, depending on which components you are working on and how much detail you go into.

A full business plan is twenty to thirty pages, plus detailed financials. If you are only updating selected sections, it will be much shorter.

Templates, styles, and formats can vary according to your business needs. In an operating business, business planning must focus on current issues and priorities, as well as taking a broad look at the market and business goals. This type of planning is for internal purposes, so your style of presentation needs to be easily understood and followed by you and others in your business. Include the appropriate level of detail to achieve it. For full business plans, use a standard template. If you are only updating sections, start with your previous versions if they were useful, or research new templates if the current one needs improvement.

If you have decided to create a complete business plan, follow any of the available standard templates that suit your needs. If you are reviewing only particular sections during your planning, you can reuse the templates you have previously used. The following templates are available from www.businessplancompany.com.au.

- Business plan
- Business goals, actions, and milestones
- Budgets and projections
- Market analysis
- Marketing plan
- Operation plan

After Your Plan Is Finished

Business planning is never "finished" whilst you own a business. For your plan to become a useful document it should be a guide you refer to as you run your business. These plans are not designed for archiving. Leaving it sitting on a shelf, gathering dust, is at best laziness and at worst self-destructive. It is important that smaller actions and tasks are taken from the plan and transferred into your weekly and monthly activities. Refer back to it, and measure your progress against the targets and strategies that are described. The format must be suitable for your business, because you need to follow it on a weekly and daily basis.

If you have completed segments of your business plan as described earlier, you need to take actions from each one and create a master action list that everyone shares and follows.

Following is an overview of a typical business review and planning schedule. Set aside regular time monthly and weekly to take a bird's-eye view of the business and at how your plans are working out. Develop key measures that will tell you whether you are on track. When your business is not doing what you planned, take time to find out what is happening and to really understand how your business and market operate. This ongoing process of learning is vital to continued growth and survival. It is a good idea to create your own "board" of interested and experienced people who can review your progress with you.

Schedule	What to Do
Annually	• Review your business plan to see how the year went in comparison to the plan. Try to understand why your business performed differently than your expectations. • Create new plans for the upcoming year. • Determine your major projects for the year, including milestones. • Set actions and tasks to achieve objectives. • Define marketing activities, budgets, and initiatives.

Monthly	• Review monthly results compared to your plan and budget.
	• Host a monthly "board" review meeting.
	• Review tasks and actions from your business plan.
	• Implement actions.
	• Review new developments.
Daily, weekly	• Review weekly results.
	• Ensure tasks, actions, and systems are implemented.
	• Ensure all activities are measured.
	• Refresh your memory on the bigger picture; measure your weekly results compared to the annual plan.

Taking words off a page and turning them into actions, accountabilities, and milestones is not too difficult to do, but it does take some discipline and forward planning. Here's how to do it.

Budgets, Projections, Sales and Other Metrics

From your projections you can take your monthly sales, costs, and profit targets and track them against actual figures each month. If you have not created sales targets within your projections, it is a good idea to do so. At your monthly board/review meeting, present analyses of business performance against your plan. Discuss variations from the plan and reasons why. If you do not have a timeline and marketing schedule/budget, consider using them; they are very useful.

Actions

As you go through your planning process, create a list of projects and actions you need to undertake as identified in your plan. Create a master list of these and then a timeline, so you can review your progress during the year.

1. For each section of your plan, identify actions you need to do. Here are some examples.

Examples

Action	
Create Facebook page	High

Action	
Job Descriptions—update	Medium

Action	
Review website	Low

2. At the end of your plan, summarise your actions, and rank them in monthly priorities with the person responsible.

Examples

July	
Create Facebook page	David
Hire new salesperson	Maria
Start new accounting system	Warren
New marketing campaign—local schools	Warren

3. Each month, add actions, with deadlines, to your calendar and/or to-do lists so they become part of your daily routine.
4. At your monthly review meeting, report on the progress of each project.

Your Plan vs. Reality

You can put whatever you like in your business plan: fast growth, great profits, and new markets; the sky is the limit. But once your business is operating and you start tracking your results against your plan, your assumptions will be tested, and you will see how accurate they are. Business planning is great for setting targets and stretch goals, but if your goals are unrealistic, your plan will become irrelevant very quickly, and you will stop using it. It's fair to say business plans, for the most part, assume your business outlook is rosier and more easily achieved than usually happens.

Here are some typical problematic examples I have seen.

- Growth targets are not realistic.
- Sales targets are too high.
- Profit margins are too high.
- Costs are forgotten or too low.
- Assumptions about the market are not accurate.
- Sales processes and times not well understood.
- Understanding of financial measures is lacking.
- Ability to achieve goals is overestimated.

If your assumptions are way off, it's a good idea to revisit your plan quickly, and revise your targets based on the updated information. Business planning is a process of reiteration; the best data you can get that will predict your future comes from your own business. By analysing all the detailed metrics in your business, you will be able to know what is reasonable and strategize how you can achieve your targets.

For more detailed instructions on how to do your business planning, go straight to part 2.

4

Business Planning for Approvals (Banks, Investors, Loans, Compliance or Licences)

In this chapter I discuss business plans that are created for a specific application or approval, such as a bank, financier, an investor, or a licence application. I call these *Plans for Others*, and it is a different exercise than business planning done solely for your own purposes.

When you are creating a plan for others, the purpose is to create a polished, professional document that tells someone else a story about your business. That person will usually know nothing about your business, and you will most likely be trying to convince them of something, like loaning you money, investing in your business, or granting you approval of some sort. The reason that you would do this type of business plan is because it is a requirement to get something that you want.

These business plans are often created more quickly, with pressure to get approvals reducing the time frame. This process is less in-depth than *Plans for Yourself*, where you select the key information to present and spend less time researching, digesting information, reviewing, thinking, and talking. You spend more time polishing the final document and less researching, which does reduce the ongoing value to your business.

Plans for Others are a subset of *Plans for Yourself*, and there can still be value in this abbreviated version of the process, as you still step away from your business (or research your new one), determine goals, budgets, understand your market, and plan for its success. In an ideal world (where you have more time) the best approach would be to create a *Plan for Yourself* and then edit it down for your application, but this rarely happens.

Your Target

Business plans for approvals are written with the audience in mind, who will have specific interests. Your plan helps them understand your application, followed by their approval or decline. It must give your reader crucial information about your business in a very short time, so it needs to be very concise. It also profiles your professionalism and preparedness, as the overall presentation of ideas, clarity, language, and professionalism give the reader a sense of who you are as an operator.

Understanding the specific requirements of the organisation granting the approval may have very specific criteria to meet. Get as much information from the authority you are submitting the plan to, obtain their guidelines, and where needed, their template. A business plan I created for a training organisation had extremely prescriptive conditions, even down to the wording of some sections that had to be copied word-for-word.

Those reviewing your plan will do so in context of your entire application, but it is a major component and tells the story of not only your business but who you are as an operator. On top of creating a description of a viable, well-planned business with sound operation and good growth opportunity, the following areas should be emphasised.

- Banks and financiers (for loan applications) want to know their loan is going to be secure and that you can comfortably service the repayments.
- Investors want to know their investment is secure, that they will get sufficient return, and when they will get their money back.
- Licences and visas will have specific criteria that are determined by the authority you are applying to.

Business Planning Process—Approvals

The business planning process is given in the following chart, with emphases on each component of the process as it applies to business plans for approvals.

1. Decide to start business planning/ write a business plan	No choice here, as it will be a prescribed component of your application.
2. Determine scope and method; select a template.	Usually there is a template suggested or prescribed.
3. Research	Medium. This is the most important part of process, but often you will need to do it more quickly to meet deadlines.
4. Document/polish	Long. When creating, polishing, and editing the plan to meet high standard or professionalism, clarity and specific criteria is a vital component.

5. Sanity check	Your business concept and proposal need rigorous checking. There may be many cycles of research-documentation-sanity check before the process is complete.
6. Submit you application	

Preparation time is usually ten to fifteen hours. However, in many cases, you will be under way with your application process by the time you start your business plan, increasing time pressures.

Plan lengths are typically ten to twenty pages, plus detailed financials. Since every business is different, the length varies enormously. Check against example plans or discuss during the sanity check, and gauge whether you need more or less detail.

Usually there will be a prescribed or recommended template and perhaps examples you should follow. Check the criteria carefully to ensure you meet the exact specifications. Keep the language and content concise, to the point, and easily understood.

Sanity Check

When your business plan is evaluated as a part of your application, it will be thoroughly assessed, analysed, and scrutinized. So it needs to be positive and paint a good picture of your business. But it also needs to be achievable, realistic, and believable. You can put whatever you want in a business plan, but if the content is not realistic, you will quickly lose credibility with your reader, and your application will be unsuccessful. Before you submit your plan, it is crucial to get an external opinion from someone who knows what they are talking about. An experienced business planner or consultant is ideal, but at the very least a family member or friend who is in business.

The ideal situation is to have an experienced small-business consultant work with you to guide you through the whole process. Business owners are often terrified of the costs of professional advice (especially new business owners), but if you get good, solid advice from an experienced consultant, it is a wise investment that can save you thousands later.

Many clients send me their business plans for editing before they submit their applications. Whilst the content can be useful most of the time, rarely is the professionalism sufficient or the level of detail completed to the required degree. Financials, which will be most scrutinized in your application, are often unrealistic.

Once Your Plan Is Finished

For your plan to become a useful document, it should become a guide you refer to as you run your business. In *Plans for Yourself*, information is included that is directly used for this purpose. These include timelines, budgets, and goals listed throughout the plan. Only some of these items—such as budgets and sales targets—are explicitly listed in *Plans for Others*, with other projects left out.

This does not mean that business plans for approvals are completely without value for steering your business during operation, but you will have to do some extra work to build the more-detailed milestones that you will need. As you are preparing your plan, keep a list of actions for yourself outside of the plan so you can develop an action plan later.

Bringing Your Plan to Life

Following is an overview of a typical business review and planning schedule. Set aside regular time monthly and weekly to take a bird's-eye view of the business, and look at how your plans are working out. Develop key measures that will tell you whether you are on track. When your business is not doing what you planned, take time to find out what is happening and to really understand how your business and market operate. This ongoing process of learning is vital to continued growth and survival. It is a good idea to create your own "board" of interested and experienced people who can review your progress with you.

Time or Event	What to Do
New business, change in direction or market/business conditions	• Create a new comprehensive business plan. • Explore current issues or changes in depth. • Create action plan and recommendations.
Annually	• Review your business plan to see how the year went in comparison to it. Try to understand why your business performed differently from your expectations. • Create a new plan for the upcoming year. • Determine your major projects for the year, including milestones. • Set actions and tasks to achieve objectives. • Define marketing activities, budgets, and initiatives.
Monthly	• Review monthly results compared to your plan and budget. • Host a monthly board/review meeting. • Review tasks and actions from your business plan. • Implement actions. • Review new developments.

Daily, weekly	• Review weekly results. • Actions from business plan • Ensure tasks, actions, and systems are being implemented. • Ensure all activities are being measured. • Refresh your memory on the bigger picture, and measure your weekly results compared to the annual plan.

Taking words off a page and turning them into actions, accountabilities, and milestones is not too difficult, but it does take some discipline and forward planning. Here's how to do it.

Budgets, Projections, Sales, and Other Metrics

From your projections you can track monthly sales, costs, and profit targets against actual each month. If you have not created sales targets within your projections, it is a good idea to do so. At your monthly board/review meeting, present analyses of business performance against your plan. Discuss variations from the plan and reasons why.

If you do not have a timeline and marketing schedule/budget, they are useful.

Actions

As you go through your planning process, create a list of projects and actions that you need to undertake as identified in your plan. Create a master list of these and then a timeline, so you can review your progress during the year.

1. For each section of your plan, identify actions that you need to do.

Examples

Action	
Create Facebook page	High

Action	
Job Descriptions—update	Medium

Action	
Review website	Low

2. At the end of your plan, summarize your actions and rank them in monthly priorities with the person responsible.

Examples

July	
Create Facebook page	David
Hire new salesperson	Maria
Start new accounting system	Warren
New marketing campaign—local schools	Warren

3. Each month, add actions to your calendar and/or to-do lists, so they become part of your daily routine; include deadlines.
4. At your monthly review meeting, report on the progress of each project.

Your Plan vs. Reality

You can put whatever you like in your business plan: fast growth, great profits, and new markets. The sky is the limit. But once your business is operating and you start tracking your results against your plan, your assumptions will be tested, and you will see how accurate they are. Business planning is great for setting targets and creating goals that stretch your business, but if your goals are unrealistic, your plan will become irrelevant very quickly, and you will stop using it. It's fair to say that business plans, for the most part, assume that your business outlook is rosier and more easily achieved than usually happens.

Some typical examples that I have seen include,

- Growth targets are not realistic.
- Sales targets are too high.
- Profit margins are too high.
- Costs are forgotten or too low.
- Assumptions about the market are not accurate.
- Sales processes and times are not well understood.
- Financial measures are poorly understood.
- Ability to achieve goals is overestimated.

Getting your assumptions right for a new business is tricky, since you have no trading history to guide you, which places a great deal of importance on the sanity check. Experienced consultants and businesspeople can tell you quickly if your proposed results are reasonable. If they come back with feedback that it is not, you will need to go back and review your assumptions.

If your assumptions are way off, it's a good idea to revisit your plan quickly and revise your targets based on the updated information. Business planning is a process of reiteration; the best data you can get that will predict your future comes from your own business. By analysing all the detailed metrics in your business, you will be able to know what is reasonable and strategize how you can achieve your targets. One of my clients starting a business in packaging manufacture was very keen to be the least expensive and had set prices very low. Once projections were completed, it was clear the business was not viable, so prices were increased.

For more detailed instructions on how to do your business planning, go straight to part 2.

Creating Your Business Plan Document

5

Before You Start Writing

Part 2 gives detailed explanations about how to write your business plan or any of the individual sections that you may create as part of your business planning. You have read the relevant chapters in Part 1 for your situation and are ready to get started. By now you understand the purpose behind planning and how the overall process looks. Before you start writing, some technical details and how-tos are explained that will help to make the process as easy as possible.

Research Methods

Getting meaningful information for your business plan needs some know-how and persistence. Big businesses have teams of analysts to dig deep; they have access to high-level reports and business analysts. In small business, as always, you will have to do it yourself. The good news is that the act of finding out information actually makes it more meaningful to you and will help transform your understanding, which can be helpful in running your business.

There is an ocean of data out there, and you could probably spend months sifting through it, but most won't be relevant or interesting to you. It is vital to know the exact questions you need answered before you even start looking. I explain specific methods as they relate to each business plan section as we go through, but for general background information, here are some useful places to start searching.

- Government agencies can have some useful big-picture data, such as industry changes, economy, population, and demographics. They can also produce useful industry reports.
- Local business groups and local councils often have reports, data on populations, council plans, traffic, and so on.
- Professional associations are good places for industry-specific news, changes, and data.
- Business networks, associations, and groups offer good information and great networks of experienced people.
- General Internet searching will uncover some interesting information, especially if you look specifically into your industry and location.
- Specialised industry reports are available, but they are usually too expensive for small businesses.
- People in your industry will already know a lot of information that will be of interest to you. If you can find someone already in your type of business from a different city or area, that is ideal.
- Looking at comparable businesses in your area, nationally or internationally, is very useful to see what works or doesn't and what your market looks like.

Case Study: New retail business

I was creating a business plan for a man who wanted to start a retail shop selling nuts. He had already found a retail premises that he was keen on, so I did some research and was lucky enough to find some data on foot traffic for that area, which was quite low. As a result of this, I recommended that he keep looking and find a site with higher traffic. Even though he would be paying more rent in a different location, his chances of success were much higher.

Case Study: Health care company

A client that provided services to the aged-care sector was looking at long-term planning, so we consulted a government report that predicted growth but also highlighted that how the sector would be funded in future would change. This helped the owners to decide on which services to focus on to ensure sustained growth.

Case Study: New medical services business

A business that provides analytical health services was looking at viability for a brand-new service not available in Australia. Since the service was most used by people with diabetes or postoperative care, we found data on both sectors, with projected numbers of the former group. These data indicated the potential for the business is very big.

Surveys

Often you won't find the exact information you need for your business, or the information available is too broad to be applicable to your specific interests. Alternatively you may be interested in market feedback on a new product or new type business. In this case, you will have to conduct some research yourself. If properly conducted, surveys give real insight into what your customers want (or might want). What I commonly see is that potential business owners ask their friends and family what they think, which, of course, is always positive. Don't do this. There are many online tools you can use to create surveys and get usable results, so if you have the time, they are well worth the effort.

If you are in business already, get someone independent to interview some of your current clients. I have done this for many clients, and it is amazingly insightful to find out what your clients really think and want. After all, what they think matters more than what you do.

Making Sense of Your Research

Research often produces a pile of data, some of it relevant, some not. Part of the planning process is sorting through it all, selecting those parts that are relevant to your business, and incorporating that information into the story of your business. This is why having a clear understanding of what you want to know ahead of your research makes this a lot easier.

To illustrate, I will use research that I completed for my own business, The Business Plan Company. Before starting the business, I wanted to know if there were enough business plans to have a viable business. Here is what happened.

1. From general reading, research, and experience, I knew that small businesses create business plans under a number of circumstances.
   Market 1: Small businesses applying for business finance and loans (mandatory)
   Market 2: Small businesses applying for business migration visas
   Market 3: Small businesses that want to plan for their future growth or start-up
2. For each market, we researched to find estimates.
   Market 1
   —Researched data on the number of business loans in Australia
   Result—2,000/year*
   Market 2
   —Spoke with a migration consultant colleague to find out which visas need business plans
   —Researched the number of the relevant visa applications per year
   Result—1,000/year*

> *Market 3*
> —*Found the number of small businesses in Australia*
> —*From personal experience, I estimated the number of small businesses that create business plans each year at 5 percent.*
> *Result*—*5 percent of 500,000 businesses = 25,000/year**
> ** Fictional numbers used.*

The Writing Process

Putting pen to paper to create your business plan can be quite daunting as you look down at a blank template, not quite knowing what to put in it. Creating the document can be done in many ways, depending on your final objectives and personal style. In general, it is best to work on one section at a time, finish it, and move on to the next one. If you find some useful information for a different section, keep it, park it into that section, and come back to it later. It's a good idea to leave notes for yourself as you go so you don't lose track of where you are or a particular detail you need to remember later.

If you encounter questions you don't know the answers to, *don't just guess*. For example, if you need a price on something, get actual quotes. If you need customer feedback, don't ask just your friends. If you need data, find it from a reputable source. Your plan needs to be based on cold, hard facts. Otherwise, your planning is meaningless.

Here is a step-by-step guide to writing your plan.

1. Collect all the information, rough notes, calculations, and research you have done so far. Add that information into the relevant sections of the template. This is very easy to do and helps build some momentum. It also shows you the "holes" in your knowledge and what you need to research.

2. Make an attempt to write the easy sections that you know, such as business description. Don't get too hung up in the early stages on having it polished; just work on the content. It will be edited later.

3. Start researching the information that you need, and add it into the plan as you go. Always add any new information into the correct section, so you can see the plan building and identify the holes. If you just dump it into a single section, you have no way of knowing how you are progressing.

4. When you feel you have enough information for one section (e.g., marketing), write the first draft of the section, even if other sections have a long way to go. Looking at a rough final product will help identify if you need more research. If needed, go back to step 3 and repeat until the section is finished to your standard. Get external input along the way if needed to check that your method or results are reasonable.

5. Repeat steps 3 and 4 until all sections are completed to your standard.

6. Give yourself a day off to clear your mind.

7. Review the whole document and check for readability, perfect formatting, consistency, and reasonableness.

8. Sanity check. Get external feedback on how realistic your business plan is.

9. If indicated by the sanity check, do additional research for some of the sections. This is not uncommon and a useful part of the process.

10. Make a final check on the edit, spellcheck, and formatting to make sure it looks great.

How Far Do You Go?

Your final business plan could be almost any length, so how do you decide how far to go into your research and how detailed you make your descriptions? It depends on the objectives of your plan and your available resources.

For *Plans for Yourself*, spend as much time as you have available, and make it as detailed as possible to create a product that you will use. Remember the point of this exercise is to improve your capability to manage the future of your business, so you need enough information to be able to do that.

For *Plans for Others*, the product must be concise, accurate, and professional, and you still need to conduct enough research to paint an accurate, realistic picture of your business. It needs to be concise so the reader quickly understands. There are many variables to consider, such as whether your business is new, whether you have a new product, if there are changes in your market, how established the business is, and how easy information is to find.

I was preparing a business plan for the purchasers of a bakery/cafe who had worked at the business for five years. Since the business had a long history, much of the content was developed from current and previous trading history. Research revolved around new marketing initiatives, local market research, and costs for expansion. In contrast, a business plan for a business importing new, environmentally friendly floor coatings required more market research, feedback from potential clients, and more-detailed financial projections, as there was little actual trading data to guide us.

Full Detail vs. Actions

When considering the level of detail for your business plan, there are two extremes.

1. Full detail, where you include a full description for that section, with all relevant information you have collected during your research. *Plans for Others* include full detail, since these plans need to be completed and polished at submission.
2. Action Item, where you list an action item, essentially means you will delay the research and implementation related to that topic until later but are noting in your business plan what you intend to do and by when. This happens because as you go through the planning process, you identify certain actions as part of your growth strategy, but it is not appropriate to do them during that time.

Examples of these two extremes could include revision of your organisational structure, revamping your website, creating marketing materials, or expanding your social media presence. All these projects take time, so you may want to add them as later projects, after the original plan is complete. Actions need to be given dates so they are completed; the action list is not a wish list but a statement of purpose. *Plans for Yourself* can include full detail and/or actions.

How to Decide What's In

As mentioned earlier, different business plan templates vary slightly in layout, structure, and emphasis, but the content is pretty much the same and is transferable. In the following chapters I endeavour to make the section names as generic as possible, so you can easily fit them into your template. Some sections are mandatory regardless of the plan; others may be longer, shorter, or omitted. Here is a guide.

Section	When and How to Include	
	Plans for Yourself	*Plans for Others*
Executive Summary	Always	Always
Introduction details	Always, full detail	Always, full detail
Business description, concept, products, and services	Always, full detail	Always, full detail
S.W.O.T.	Always	Always
Legal/Regulation/ Insurance/ Compliance	Always. Level of detail will vary with type of business and whether start-up or operating.	Summary, focusing on those relevant to application
Location/venue/ facility	Always. More detail for new businesses or change to current.	Always. Short summary
History	Not always; where relevant.	Always, to build case for application. Concise
Market	Always. Level of detail will vary with type of business and whether start-up or operating. Some elements may be included as actions	Always. Concise summary as relevant to application
Business goals/ growth targets	Always. Level of detail will vary depending of start-up/ operating business	Always. Concise summary as relevant to application.

Marketing	Always. Level of detail will vary a lot. Quite common that elements will be included as actions.	Always. Short summary
Sales	Always. Level of detail will vary a lot. Quite common that elements will be included as actions	Not often. Short summary if pertinent to application.
Operations	Always. Detailed, especially for new businesses or changes to operation. Quite common that elements will be included as actions	Always. Short summary
Regulations, legal, compliances, and insurances	Always. Detailed, especially for new businesses or changes to operation.	Always. Short summary
Equipment and infrastructure	Included for new businesses or changes to operation.	Not always. Short summary as relevant to application.
People	Always. For very small businesses, this will be a short statement of responsibilities. Detail varies with size of business and whether start-up or operating. Quite common that elements will be included as actions.	Always. Concise description.
Risks	Always	Always

Sourcing, procurement, inventory, and logistics	Always. Detail varies with size of business and whether start-up or operating. Quite common that elements will be included as actions	Short summary as relevant to application.
Timeline	Not always for operating businesses, depending on upcoming business activities. Always for new businesses.	As relevant to application.
Website and Internet	Always Detail varies with size of business and whether start-up or operating. Quite common that elements will be included as Actions	As relevant to application.
IT	Not always for operating businesses, depending on upcoming business activities. Always for new businesses.	As relevant to application.
Financials— projections, cash flow, balance sheet, and break even	Projections (P&L) and summary—always. Balance sheet and cash flow—as required by the authority.	Projections (P&L) and summary—always. Balance sheet and cash flow—as required by the authority.
Financial—start-up costs/project costs	Not always for operating businesses, depending on upcoming business activities. Always for new businesses.	As relevant to application.
Action plan	Always	Summary when is essential part of business growth story.
Appendix/references	Always	Always

The Sections: Executive Summary

6

The Executive Summary often feels quite daunting to write, because it needs to be concise and compelling. Ironically, it is probably the easiest section to write if you follow a very simple process. This is essentially a one- or two-page summary of the plan that allows the reader to get a clear understanding of your business proposal in a very short time. The reader can then read on for more detail if he or she wants to.

Executive summaries are always found in *Plans for Others*. If you are creating a *Plan for Yourself*, this section is not always mandatory, since it is usually only read internally. In fact, I commonly leave it out of these plans. An Executive Summary would never be listed as an action.

What to Do

1. Finish your business plan; this section is written at the end, once the rest is complete.
2. Copy and paste the entire business plan into a new document, and save it as a separate file.
3. Sequentially delete information from the entire document to pare it down to a one- or two-page summary of the most essential information. Make sure to include enough

so the reader will still understand the whole story of the plan. This sounds easy enough, but the skill is deciding which parts are essential. Keep the purpose of your plan in mind as you edit. For example, if it is a finance application for a new business, you need to tell readers it is a new business, when it will start, and why it will succeed.

Here are some guidelines.

- Delete obviously nonessential sections, like references, organisational charts, and S.W.O.T.
- Change formatting of each chapter to remove numbering, and use each chapter as a section heading for the Executive Summary. You can leave the most essential headings in the final version; delete the rest towards the end of the edit.
- The first two paragraphs or overview sections often contain the core essence of what you are communicating in your plan, so use those and edit to just bare-bones information.
- Financials are mandatory, but just include summaries, such as total start-up or project costs and annual summaries of revenue/costs/profits.
- Marketing should be included as short overview and brief list of initiatives.

4. Edit the whole Executive Summary to make sure it reads well.

5. Insert your finished Executive Summary back into the original business plan.

Example: Training Company

Executive Summary

ABC Training is a new training company that will provide nationally accredited certificates in fence building, axe grinding, tyre changing, and window cleaning. This is in addition to professional development training for the trade sector. We provide training to high school graduates, industry groups, and unemployed jobseekers. In addition to our training facilities, we have a team of trainers ready to provide on-site tailored courses. ABC Training is flexible, efficient, and offers hassle-free training to meet trainee's needs. ABC Training will conduct training at our dedicated training facility or at our client's location as required.

Values

As a committed, professional organisation, ABC Training focuses on the training and services that it provides to our clients through professionally measurable results. We are able to add value to all our clients through quality-driven human resources and quality products which all add significant value to our clients and the client's business operations.

We will do this through high-quality teaching from industry-experienced trainers, a diverse range of courses, nationally accredited qualifications, flexible study options, and technology.

Clients

The target market for ABC Training includes

- Cleaners
- Trades
- High school leavers
- Unemployed jobseekers

Operations

ABC Training is currently in set-up phase and is seeking a premises in north-western Melbourne. Training materials are already developed. The ABC Training team, which will include two owners, has vast experience in administration, management, training, and assessment. In addition to this, well-qualified and experienced staff will be hired when business starts operation.

Marketing

ABC Training has created a marketing strategy to grow our business, student numbers, and profile. Marketing initiatives will include advertisements, educational agents (in Australia and international), relationships with allied organisations, trade shows, online marketing, sponsorship, referrals, and social media.

Financial Projections

The total set-up cost to start ABC Training is $92,000, all of which is currently held and available. A summary of profit and loss projections is shown below.

	2019-20	2020-21
Total revenue	$587,300.00	$632,500.00
Total cost of sales	$158,398.30	$160,898.20
Gross profit	$428,901.70	$471,601.80
Total costs	$135,140.04	$135,140.04
Net profit (loss)	$293,761.66	$436,461.76

7

The Sections:
Business Information
and Description

This introductory section sets the scene for your business plan and clearly identifies who you are and what you do. Keep this information factual, without trying to influence the reader too much. This section is mandatory in all business plans.

I explain in more detail each part of this section, but here are some general guidelines.

	Plans for Yourself	*Plans for Others*
Start-up business	Describe in detail, as this will help you to clarify to yourself.	Describe in very concise language with enough detail for the reader to understand at a higher level.
Operating business	Revise your previous description, and refine as needed. Can be shorter.	Describe in very concise language with enough detail for the reader to understand at a higher level.

Here are some common problems I see in this section.

- Not explaining what your business does, because there is too much information or not presented clearly enough.
- Overselling the benefits of the product or service. This should occur in later sections.
- Overcomplicating the descriptions.
- For new and novel products and services, not comparing them to those already offered, so the reader has difficulty placing your product in the market.

Business Description/Concept

In this section, describe your business at a higher level. It will include such things as the type of business (e.g., restaurant), what industry you are in (e.g., property services), and the area you will service (e.g., southern California). You can also include a brief statement about your point of difference. If your business is a new idea or concept, you may need to go into further detail to explain it, but always edit to minimize the number of words. In order to get concise and correct descriptions, look at those of similar businesses.

Examples

<Business Name> is a digital technology company offering computer development services, currently server and Web applications. Inspired by and modelled on <Inspiring Business Name>, a US-based technology company that has built a brand around strength in technological expertise.
With over fifteen years development experience, <Business Name> specializes in solving difficult problems and bringing the solutions to market when our clients do not have the expertise to do so, removing the technical headaches through developing websites and apps to get products to market quickly and painlessly.

<Business Name> is a new training company that will provide nationally accredited certificates in education and health care, in addition to

professional development training for the early childhood sector. We provide training and education to the community and business groups. In addition to our training facilities, we have a team of trainers ready to provide on-site tailored courses. <Business Name 2> is flexible, efficient, and offers hassle-free training to meet trainee's needs. <Business Name 2> will conduct training at our dedicated training facility of at our client's location as required.

<Business Name> is a well-established food and beverage business located in the High St Happyville shopping strip. The business has operated for more than thirty years under different names and owners, with the current owners in place for approximately five years. With such a long history, there is an established client base with loyal regular customers. <Business Name> trades seven days per week for breakfast and lunch.

Products/Services

This section extends on the business description/concept by adding more detail about specific products or services that the business will offer. Again, keep it as concise as you can, but give enough detail so the reader will be able to understand later sections, where you describe financials, operations, and marketing. If your product is new or novel, you may need to describe in more detail, describe similar businesses (sometimes international) or where your products and services fit into those currently available in the market. Expect to include up to one page.

<Business Name> provides career management and development services to assist professionals improve their career prospects. The process usually involves three broad stages.
1. Getting the focus. Investigations of personal style, key skills, and values. From this personal insight, the development of a career vision that satisfies the needs and values of the participant.
2. Preparation. Activities which prepare the participant to embark on the job search: updating resume, techniques of job searching, managing, and job search and interview skills.
3. Action. Implementation of the plan evolved from steps 1 and 2, and finding the most rewarding role or business to start.

Objectives for participants are
> *finding a rewarding career path*
> *evaluating key strengths*
> *identifying development needs*
> *increasing career options*

Each stage has a number of potential components, as shown below. Programs are tailored to meet the exact needs of individual clients, so the components included in each program will vary.

<Business Name> is a bakery-style café that has established a reputation for baked foods (excluding breads) and coffee. It is famous for pies, cakes, and other pastry items. Currently selling 10kg coffee/week. Customers purchase as takeaway (70 percent of sales) or sit-down (30 percent).
Current menu:

• *pie varieties*	• *quiche varieties*	• *cake varieties*
• *sausage rolls*	• *spinach rolls*	• *party foods*
• *Danishes*	• *croissants*	• *scones*
• *fruit pies*	• *fruit tarts*	• *vanilla slices*
• *lemon tarts*	• *éclairs*	• *hedgehog slices*
• *shortbread biscuits*	• *ginger bread biscuits*	• *various biscuit varieties*
• *soft drinks*	• *coffee*	• *milkshakes and sandwiches.*

Future menu additions:
• *sandwiches, focaccias, and freshly squeezed juices.*
• *catering*
• *expansion of birthday cakes, particularly as marketing driver*

<Business Name> will provide four courses:
Anaphylaxis/Asthma—combined first-aid management of anaphylaxis
This course will assist students in learning how to assess situations for anaphylaxis, provide appropriate treatment for anaphylactic reaction, identify individuals at risk of allergic reactions and anaphylaxis, and develop individual anaphylaxis management plans.
This course is recognised by the XXXX as fulfilling the requirements for asthma and anaphylaxis training.
Course code: XXXXX

Emergency Management of Asthma in the Workplace
This course covers the knowledge and skills to recognise the clinical manifestations of asthma and identify and respond to an asthma emergency. Students will learn symptoms and triggers of an asthma attack, medications, and the devices used to administer them.

This course is recognised by the Australian Children's Education and Care Quality Authority (ACECQA) as fulfilling the requirements for asthma and anaphylaxis training.
Course code: XXXXX
Price: $10

First-Aid Course
The first-aid course is nationally recognised and aligns with the policies of the Australian Resuscitation Council (ARC). Students learn the skills and gain the knowledge required to provide first-aid response, life support, and management of casualty(ies), the incident, and other first-aiders until the arrival of medical or other assistance. These skills and knowledge may be applied in a range of situations, including community and workplace settings.
Course code: XXXXX
Price: $1,000

Child-Care Services Certificate III
The Certificate III in children's services meets the needs of the children's services sector. The course trains students to become early-childhood educators, who plan and provide child care and education for infants and children up to twelve years of age.
Students will be equipped with the necessary skills to use organisational policies and procedures, and individual children's profiles to supervise activities and provide care for children.
Code: XXXX
Price: $5,000

History/Progress

The story of every business is different, and this section aims to quickly take the reader through your story to the present. The purpose is to build a stronger case around your experience and motivation for the particular business, and to give assurance that the progress to date in your business and/or life brings strengths to your business proposition. You would expect this section to be about a page in length, unless there are specific details that give weight to your proposal. You may leave this section out for a *Plan for Yourself* (since it is only used internally), but it is mandatory for *Plans for Others*.

There are many variations in content, depending on your situation, but here are some guidelines.

- *New businesses* should state that the business is new and has no trading history, but include information about the business owner's history that builds confidence in the likelihood of success. Speak also of your motivation for the business and where you saw the opportunity. It is also a good idea to include a brief summary Curriculum Vitae (CV) in the appendix of all decision-makers and directors.
- *Operating businesses* should give a brief overview of the business history, including such details as time in business, financials, successes, trading history, and major developments. If there is any change occurring at the time of the plan—such as sale of the business, new contract, and so on—this needs to be clearly explained.

Example: New Business

<Business Name> is a new business and has no trading history. However, principal John has extensive experience in the property sector and property recruitment. Relevant previous experience:
October 2007-June 2010

Previous Employer, Senior Property Consultant
- *Executive search, permanent and temporary recruitment in the property space in Victoria, specializing in sales, marketing, and retirement. Established a new desk to an average billing of $30Kpcm*
- *Major clients include ...*

2007

Business Name. Estate Manager
- *Manning of sale and information centres of respective estates*
- *Dealing with all enquiries and sales-related matters from initial enquiry through to sale of land*
- *Liaising with local builder networks to establish appropriate house and land packages and referral networks with regards to the relevant development*
- *Attending relevant developer meetings where required*
- *Researching and preparing weekly and monthly activity and competition reports*

2005-2006
<Business Name> Entrepreneur
- *Business planning/concept design*
- *Advertising/marketing*
- *Financial management*
- *Operations management*

Example: New Car Wash

Business Name> is a new business that is in the advance stages of planning. There is no trading history. The following stages of the development of the site and business have been completed.

Negotiation of price for purchase of land

Purchase of land, subject to successful financing and acquisition of necessary plans and permits

Development of architectural plans

Assessment and recommendations by town planner

Submission of plans to council for approval of subdivision and planning approval for construction

Selection of builder; final prices are still being negotiated.

The business owners have been employees at <Car Wash 1> for five years. Please find CVs included in appendix x.

Location/Venue/Facility/Premises

This section is dedicated to the description of the place where you will conduct business. The objective is to paint a visual picture where you do (or will do) business, the foundation for your operations, and the impact that it has on your business. This includes details about the actual premises and location and any pertinent local information or changes that are happening, as well as the impacts they will have on your business. These details help the reader to visualise your business and provides valuable background that helps to understand marketing and financials in later sections.

You might include such details as

- location;
- impact of location if it is relevant, such as position in a retail strip or part of an industrial estate or business hub;
- features of the location that are of interest to the business, such as access to transport links, views, or business facilities;
- other relevant location information that helps to build the business case, such as traffic numbers or growth predictions for the area;
- features of the premises itself that are of interest to the particular business, such as a kitchen or permits for a restaurant, fast Internet, and so on;
- plans to develop the premises or renovate;
- details such as floor plans if they are relevant;
- fit-out and fixtures; and
- council plans and permits.

The length and detail will depend on your situation. In *Plans for Yourself*, the level of detail is quite flexible. For new businesses, go into more detail, as it helps to build a comprehensive picture of your business that will help you prepare. If your business is already operating, only changes need to be included; for example a new premises, renovations, or identified needs for change/upgrade.

In *Plans for Others*, include information that is of interest to your business proposal, as detailed previously. Remember the reader has no idea about your business, so you need to take him or her there in your plan.

Example

Premises and Location

<Business Name> is currently leasing a factory within the Business Park area, Main Rd., Dandenong South.

The property boasts to full access to interchanges of EastLink via Greens Road and Dandenong Bypass. The location provides nonstop linkages to all major freeways and arterials in Melbourne. Floor plans are shown in appendix 2. Features include

- High exposure
- Double-storey office
- Dual RSDs
- Drive-through facility
- Secure rear yard
- Secure premises with electric gates
- Zoned Industrial 1
- Floor space 700m^2
- Racking already installed
- Three-phase power

The current lease extends two years from the date of this plan. It is anticipated that growth goals described in this plan will require a larger facility at the end of the current lease.

Premises and Location

<Business Name> is located at 17 Funny St., Lala Land, approximately 11km west of Melbourne GPO. Funny St. is an established suburban shopping strip with over one hundred local businesses, a local traders group, and significant vehicle traffic. Businesses along the strip include

- Fresh food
- Fashion
- Hair and beauty
- Banks
- Leisure, learning, and lifestyle
- Professional services

- Cafes and takeaway
- Gifts
- Health
- Supermarkets and Variety
- Real estate
- Supplies

Further information:

Lala Land shopping centre: www.lalashopping.com.au/

Local Trader's Association: www.website.com.au

SWOT

SWOT is a well-established, structured, planning method used in all business plans to evaluate the strengths, weaknesses, opportunities, and threats involved in the business. In essence, it is a very short, powerful summary of internal and external factors that work in favour and against the business. This section is mandatory and needs to be completed in all plans and reviews.

- Strengths are *internal* characteristics of the business that are favourable to achieving goals.
- Weaknesses are *internal* characteristics of the business that are not favourable to achieving goals.
- Opportunities are *external* factors that are favourable to achieving goals.
- Threats are *external* factors that are not favourable to achieving goals.

Example

Strengths
- *Unique product range*
- *Site secured in favourable location*
- *High profit margins*
- *Previous industry experience and contacts of owners*
- *Strong support team of advisers*

Weaknesses
- *No previous experience operating a small business*
- *Managing cash flow, due to long payment cycles*
- *Reliance on small number of suppliers which can be unreliable*
- *High pressure to generate immediate return*
- *Compliance requirements are time consuming*

Opportunities
- *Current industry growth*
- *Further product sales to existing*
- *Franchise development*
- *Increase in online sales*
- *Changes in government legislation to liberalise market*

Threats
- *Currency rates may affect prices or reduce profit margins.*
- *Competitors could easily move into the market, especially those better resourced.*
- *New technology developments that change marketplace*
- *Availability of suitably qualified staff*

What to Do

- As you go through your business planning, make notes of SWOTs as they occur. Expect to finalize your SWOT list at the end of your planning, as more will crop up as you go through the process.
- Download a template that has suggested SWOT items to generate thoughts about your own business (available at www.businessplancompany.com.au). From this list, keep those that are relevant and customize to accurately describe your own business.
- Edit your SWOT to ensure language is concise and you have a list of the five or six most important points for each category.

Legals, Regulations, Insurances, and Compliance

Every business operates within an environment where rules and regulations must be adhered to in order to trade. These could include a vast array of compliances as diverse as food handling, professional registrations, police checks, liquor licensing, environmental laws, and local council. Every business will be different, but such compliances can have a big effect on your business operations, viability, and profitability. This section does not refer to taxation compliances, which require involvement of an accountant. This section is mandatory for all business plans.

If you are already operating, you will know what these are already, so their inclusion in your planning might revolve more around how to manage them better or reviews that may be required.

Ultimately, it is your responsibility to know your obligations, so thorough research is needed. At a minimum, you should

- Contact all levels of government to find out what regulations affect your business and how to comply.
- Speak to owners of similar businesses.
- Contact an insurance broker or company to find out what insurances you should have and those that you may consider.
- Get legal advice.
- Contact professional associations.
- Consult an accountant.
- Check your agreements and contracts for compliance conditions.

Examples

- *<Business Name> will require annual police checks for all staff who provide services. These will be managed by administration assistant, who will maintain a schedule to ensure they are always valid.*
- *Liquor licenses are currently held at our premises and are current until November 30, 2020. This is managed by CEO and will be renewed before this date.*
- *Business Name holds public liability Insurance for $20M and professional indemnity insurance for $5M with Insurance Company X. All policies are renewed annually on June 30. See appendix for Certificate of Currency.*

Actions
- *Contact insurance broker to review insurances before June 1.*
- *Complete food handling certificate for all team members by July 28.*
- *Create employment contracts for employees by November 30.*

Example: Consulting Company

Regulatory Requirements
- *Business Name is required to comply with the following legislation and regulatory requirements, which are addressed in the quality manual for the organisation. Information regarding individual responsibilities and obligations is shared with clients, staff, and students through appropriate handbooks and material.*
- *Quality framework*
- *Competition and Consumer Act*
- *Copyright*
- *Privacy Act*
- *Workplace health and safety*
- *Access and equity*

Insurance
Business Name will hold the following insurances.
- *Public liability*
- *Professional indemnity*
- *Workers compensation insurance*
- *Contents insurance*

The Sections:
The Numbers

8

In most business plans you will find sections dedicated to financials, growth, targets, and other metrics located in different sections. To my mind, these are part of the same topic, so I prefer to add them all in the same section I call "The Numbers." You can include many metrics in this section, including sales forecasts, pricing, and margins; the financials will still form a significant part.

Common problems I see with this section include the following:

- Projections and budgets have not been developed with enough research, so they are not accurate nor reflect actual costs.
- Projections are not realistic, such as margins too high, revenue growth too ambitious, or margins not achievable.
- Ratios are not realistic, so they raise suspicions about the accuracy of the overall projections.
- No data is provided to back up the projections.
- Assumptions are not stated.
- Start-up costs are not well researched and/or omit obvious costs.
- For those plans seeking financiers or investors, not enough detail is provided about what you will do with the investment and how profit/repayments will be distributed/made.

Pricing

Describing your pricing structure in your planning sets the foundation for all financials in the rest of your plan, as well as guides the reader to where your products and services are positioned in the market. By including this information, you are presenting a more complete picture of your business.

Inclusion of pricing in your plans will be in accordance with the following:

- *Plans for Others* will include a short statement or grid that lists your prices and, where needed, an explanation of any peculiarities that need explanation. Keep it short and succinct.
- In *Plans for Yourself,* include full details for new businesses and only details for operating businesses where there is some kind of review needed. It is fine to include a pricing review as actions for these plans.

Example: Health-Consulting Business

Pricing Structure		
Type of Test	*Duration*	*Price*
Test 1	15 minutes	$79 ($71.81 + GST)
Test 2	15 minutes	$99 ($90 + GST)
Test 3	30 minutes	$148.50 ($135 + GST)
Test 4	30 minutes	$148.50 ($135 + GST)
Test 5	30 minutes	$99 ($90 + GST)
Test 6	15 minutes	$79 ($71.81 + GST)

Start-Up Costs/Project Costs

Starting a business costs money. The lowest cost might be a sole operator in a home-based consulting business, with such inclusions as minimal infrastructure, marketing, website, and insurances. The highest cost is as high as your budget permits and could include buildings, vehicles, inventory, staff, marketing, and equipment; the sky is the limit. Despite perceptions of many aspiring business owners, starting a business is not completely free. Similarly with business growth projects, they all require some investment.

Before you take the leap into starting a business or project, you need to know how much it is going to cost. Not only can you decide whether you have enough money or whether you need to source more financing, it gives you power to control the budget once you start.

Unless you have been in business before, you won't be aware of all the costs you can incur and will likely omit certain things. Things like insurances, accounting set-up fees, and legal set-up fees are frequently forgotten in start-up cost estimates. The biggest cost that is unaccounted for, however, is the money you will need to live on before your business generates a profit.

Low Budget Start-Ups

When you are starting on a low budget, you need to know in accurate detail everything that may come up and how much it will cost, so you can carefully plan how to stretch your limited budget. To keep your start-up costs down, be prepared to roll up your sleeves. Using your own time is the easiest trade-off for not spending money. You may also need to call in some favours from people you know or come up with other novel ways to pay for the services of others. Exchanging services is effective. For example, two of my clients exchanged financial advice and web design.

What to Do

Start with a template that lists a wide range of costs, so you don't forget anything. (There is one available at businessplancompany. com.au). I cannot emphasise enough the importance of getting actual costs when you are doing this exercise. Take your time, and *don't just guess*.

1. Start with a template that lists all of the possible start-up costs that you could incur.
2. Go through each of the list items and mark in the first column whether you need that item or not. Make notes as you go.

Since spreadsheets with financial data are large documents with a lot of entries, a working example is not possible to fit into this book. Please download some examples from businessplancompany. com.au and work through these as you read this chapter.

3. Once you have decided what you need, find actual prices for all those things, putting those prices in the "Estimated Cost" column. Update the notes as you go, so you remember how you arrived at that price or who the supplier is.
4. Review each of your estimated costs with an experienced businessperson to see if they are reasonable.
5. Calculate the total and then review your financial position and each item. You may need to make some alterations to fit items into your budget, source more funds, or wait until you have more funds.

There may be items on your list that you decide to pay for once you generate some cash flow. This is a risky proposition, since you have no guarantee of any cash flow. Keep those items to a minimum.

What to Put in Your Plan

Include a summary of costs in the body of the plan with full details in the appendices. This section needs to be done before beginning a new business and is not suitable to be included as an action. If you are an operating business that is analysing future business projects, it is fine to include as an action so long as it is complete before you start the project.

Business Goals/Growth Targets

This is a short summary section that gives key numbers, usually by financial year. Think of it as a "headline" section that gives the reader just the base numbers in order to set the scene. This section is essential in every business plan and does need to be completed in your initial plan.

Financials would include

- revenue;
- gross profit;
- overhead; and
- operating/net profit.

In addition, you would also include key sales and client data relevant to your business, such as

- total number of sales;
- total number of clients;
- average sales;
- sales by product or service type; and
- sales by region, state, or country.

Caution

In your plans, this section is included first to be consistent with the development of your business story, but it should actually be entered after you have completed detailed projections (which are included in a later section). These numbers need to be a summary of those projections and must be exactly the same.

Example: Start-Up Business

<Business Name> will start trade in the Melbourne area, aiming at clusters of clients in areas local to business operations, particularly Melbourne's eastern suburbs, Mornington Peninsula and inner Melbourne Bayside.

Stage 1, six to twelve months, establishment

In the early stages, focus will be on establishing processes, IT systems, building the team, and building understanding around client needs and satisfaction.

Stage 2, six to twelve months and longer, rapid growth

Once systems have been established and business owners are feeling confident in scalability, resources will be focused on growing team of agents and client base.

Growth Targets

	1 Year	*2 Years*
Business revenue	$546K	$1.99M
Operating profit	$187K	$725K
Number of clients	75	143
Agents	75	143

Projections: Profit and Loss (P&L)

Projections are detailed, month to month estimates of business finances, including all sales, costs, and profits. Although they are an estimate, the process of creating projections is extremely valuable, as it makes you look at every detail of your business. Even those of you who are afraid of numbers, make the effort to do this. You will understand your business so much better once you have finished. Get help if you need it.

The most common type of projections are P&L based on accruals, meaning the entries are made the month that they are incurred, rather than when cash comes in and goes out of your business. An example follows. It can feel daunting when you are first presented with the task of creating projections, but there are logical steps to follow. Do them step by step, and you will learn the methodology. This section needs to be completed in your initial plan and is not suitable to be included as an action.

What to Do

1. Template

Start with a projection template for small business. (You can find one at www.thebusinessplancompany.com.au.) In it are three sections: "Revenue," "Cost of Sales," and "Overheads." Those labels may vary depending on which template you use. The process involves working through each of these line-by-line, adding entries for the next one or two years. For operating businesses, twelve monthly projections are adequate. However, it is common to create longer projections for new businesses or for specific applications. Keep in mind the longer the time frame of the projections, the less certain they become.

One additional column in the template is the Assumptions column. When you enter data into each of the categories, add your reasons for adding those values in this column, for example, "$50/month, $1,500 paid in October, or 9.5 percent of salaries." It's very easy to forget your assumptions, so be disciplined about adding them in. It also makes sanity check easier. If you are in business already, your previous financial statements will give you the most accurate source information. Get a copy of your P&L expressed monthly to use as a starting point.

2. Sales/Income/Revenue

Estimating can be done in two different ways.

Method 1. Make an estimate of total sales. This is the easy method but is likely to be less accurate, as it is not linked to detailed sales targets. It is more an estimation than breakdown of your assumptions. When doing so, you need to be mindful of seasonal variations as well as growth targets. Religious festivals, school holidays, summer, and winter, for example, all affect businesses in different ways.

For example, see below for sales estimates based on a 5 percent increase year-on-year for a timber coatings business I worked with. Totals for the next year 2 are simply 5 percent more than the previous year.

	Year 1	Year 2
July	$198,000	$207,900
August	$210,000	$220,500
September	$216,000	$226,800
October	$235,000	$246,750
November	$252,000	$264,600
December	$265,000	$278,250

January	$157,000	$164,850
February	$210,000	$220,500
March	$212,000	$222,600
April	$258,000	$270,900
May	$260,000	$273,000
June	$298,000	$312,900
Total	**$2,771,000**	**$2,909,550**

Method 2. Divide your revenue into different classes of product or service and then work out a sales budget based on expected numbers of clients and average sales. This method is more accurate, because it is based on a deeper analysis of sales and prices rather than just a total sales target. It also develops your sales budget at the same time.

For example, let's say you have two products. Product X sells for an average of $150, and Product Y sells for an average of $900. In the following example, monthly sales numbers are based on your estimations or previous sales. Product X is an older product that is phasing out and declining in sales; product Y is newer and increasing, with price rises marked for the start of the next year. Total revenue is the product of those numbers.

It is always better to use method 2, but the type of business can make this more challenging. In businesses with a broad or complex product range, such as retail or a restaurant, you may have to divide your products or services into classes, such as food and beverage or state by state.

Please download working examples at <u>businessplancompany.com.au</u>

3. Cost of Sales

This is the second part of the projections template and includes all costs you incurred to create your product or service, such as ingredients or materials, machinery, and wages for either production or services. Often these are expressed as a percentage of your sale price or a cost per unit. Add the appropriate formulas to automatically calculate the costs and totals. If you are in business already use the ratios from your previous financial statements. If you are new to business, getting professional help or finding industry standard ratios.

Gross profit (GP) = sales – total cost of sales. Check that the formulas are working. Knowing GP as a percentage of total sales is also very useful.

4. Overheads

These are costs that are more consistent and not tightly linked to levels of business, sales, or production. These costs include insurance, marketing, rent, accounting costs, and support staff wages. Enter all costs for each month of the year. For example, rent is paid each month and insurance in October. Do your best to get the months correct, as this has an impact on your final result.

If you have been in business before, you can look at last year's costs as a good approximation for the upcoming year, making adjustments for changes in costs. For new businesses, getting accurate costs will require work to get the best estimates of costs and times. Use the overhead costs to then calculate your operating profit.

5. Sanity Check

Go through your estimated cost list with an experienced businessperson and review your assumptions to see if they are reasonable. Finally, calculate the totals and look at how much money you will make (or lose). This can be a big reality check, but it helps to align you with how your business will operate. If the numbers seem unreal, the person reviewing your application will probably think so too, so go back through your assumptions again.

Once you have it complete, play around with the numbers to see what happens when you increase sales, decrease costs, and so on. It's very useful to see how your business financials work on paper. For example, you may have to increase your sales targets, sell more, or look at ways of cutting costs.

What to Put in Your Plan

Normally you would put a summary of sales, cost of sales, and operating profit per year in the body of the plan. Full details will be included in the in the Appendix.

	Revenue	GP	Operating Profit
Year 1	$156,765.00	$144,765.00	$17,996.30
Year 2	$268,505.00	$246,005.00	$75,992.70
Year 3	$435,953.00	$358,453.00	$143,514.00

Projections: Balance Sheet

Balance sheet projections and summaries in business planning are generally included when they are required specifically for a particular application (with a *Plan for Others*). Businesses that are more advanced in their financial analyses will also include them. Having a good understanding of your business' balance sheet is vital. Working closely with your accountant to develop and explain them is vital to their accuracy due to their complexity. This section does not need to be completed in your initial plan (unless specified) and is suitable to be included as an action.

What to Do

- For *Plans for Others*, check the specifications for the plan.
- Create your P&L projections and then give them to your accountant.
- If you want/need to create balance sheet projections, your accountant will be able to help you put them together.

What to Put in Your Plan

Normally, you would put a summary into the body of your plan, with full details included in the Appendix. For *Plans for Others*, you may have very specific templates and tables in which to input data.

Example: Technology company

Balance Sheet Forecast	Year 1	Year 2	Year 3
Current Assets			
Cash	$5,996.30	$21,989.00	$75,503.00
Accounts receivable	$0	$0	$0
Inventory	$0	$0	$0
Total current assets	$5,996.30	$21,989.00	$75,503.00
Fixed Assets			
Fixed assets	$0	$0	$0
Less accumulated depreciation	$0	$0	$0

Net fixed assets	$0	$0	$0
Current Liabilities			
Accounts payable	$66,056.00	$84,444.00	$118,433.00
Deferred revenue	$643.00	$1,284.00	$2,715.00
Short-term debt	$0	$0	$0
Total current liabilities	$66,699.00	$85,728.00	$121,148.00
Long-Term Liabilities			
Long-term loans	$0	$0	$0
Total capital	$5,996.30	$21,989.00	$75,503.00
Totals			
Total assets	$5,996.30	$21,989.00	$75,503.00
Total liabilities and capital	$72,695.30	$107,717.00	$196,651.00

Projections: Cash Flow

P&L projections are the standard method for creating projections, but there are many factors that will impact the amount of cash available. Since cash is the lifeblood of any business, being aware of cash flowing in and out is a useful additional projection to have. Cash flow projections are not as common in *Plans for Yourself* but are well worth the extra time taken to add them in, as you can see ahead whether you will have sufficient cash to keep operating. In *Plans for Others*, they would usually be specified as needed.

Cash flow impacts are included as an addition to your P&L statement and show those financial movements that are not completed in the month they start (and are recorded in your P&L). This typically includes

- Client payments have longer or staged payment cycles.
- Payments made on a period longer than monthly, for example, superannuation and taxes.

- Payments made to your suppliers that have delayed payments.
- Wages and salaries not paid monthly.

Cash	2014	2014	2014	2014
GST	Jul	Aug	Sep	Oct
GST collected	$ 1,910.00	$ 340.00	$ 360.00	$ 3,960.00
GST credits	$ 567.72	$ 409.87	$ 409.97	$ 639.57
BAS Payment or Tax Payment				$ 1,222.45
GST - effect on cash	$ 1,342.28	-$ 69.87	-$ 49.97	$ 2,097.98

Superannuation	Jul	Aug	Sep	Oct
Paid				$ 855.00
Superanunation - effect on cash	$ -	$ 285.00	$ 570.00	-$ 95.00

Salary	Jul	Aug	Sep	Oct
Salary - effect on cash	$ -	$ -	$ -	$ -

Cash	Jul	Aug	Sep	Oct
Open Bank	$6,150.00	$16,053.45	$8,211.64	-$2,411.26
Net cash in/out	$ 9,903.45	-$ 7,841.81	-$ 10,622.91	$ 20,271.78
Shareholder Loans				
Fitout & Equipment				
Balance end of month	$ 16,053.45	$ 8,211.64	$ (2,411.26)	$ 17,860.51

What to Do

- Create your P&L projections.
- Consult with your accountant to clarify which items have an impact on your cash, and add these items into the cash section of the projections template.

What to Put in Your Plan

For *Plans for Yourself*, develop the additional calculations in the same template you used to calculate P&L. You may choose not to add them into the body of the plan. If you decide that you will undertake cash flow projections as a later project, schedule it early in your timeline. It is common to identify finance needs as a result of doing cash projections, so further actions may also be generated. For *Plans for Others*, the inclusion of cash flow projections will be as a summary (usually annual), often with a specified template to follow.

Example: Cash Flow Summary for BP

Cash Flow Forecast	YEAR 1	YEAR 2	YEAR 3
Cash In			
Sales	$156,765.00	$276,005.00	$448,453.00
Other income	$0	$0	$0
Loans	$0	$0	$0
Investments	$0	$0	$0
Total Cash In	$156,765.00	$276,005.00	$448,453.00
Cash Out			
COGS	$12,000.00	$30,000.00	$90,000.00
Other expenses	$66,056.00	$84,444.00	$118,433.00
Payroll	$65,000.00	$83,000.00	$125,000.00
Cash paid for taxes	$7,712.70	$32,568.30	$61,506.00
Cash paid for fixed assets	$0	$30,000.00	$0
Loan principal payments	$0	$0	$0
Loan interest payments	$0	$0	$0
Owner's draws and dividends	$0	$0	$0
Total Cash Out	$150,768.70	$260,012.30	$394,939.00
Net and Balance			
Starting cash balance	$0	$0	$0
Net cash flow	$5,996.30	$15,992.70	$53,514.00
Ending Cash Balance	$5,996.30	$21,989.00	$75,503.00

Financial Ratios

Some *Plans for Others* require the inclusion of specific financial ratios in their business plans, which could include ratios such as

- Net profit (loss) ratio
- Sales and service to total income

- Net profit to tangible assets
- Working capital
- Cash to current assets
- Current assets to total assets
- Current liabilities to total liabilities
- Debt to equity ratio

What to Do

Ratios are easy to calculate once your P&L projections and balance sheet projections are complete. These ratios are only required when specified by the authority you are submitting your application to. They will require these data to be presented using the specified format. Check the template or specifications.

Section 4

Ratios Table 1

Profitability And Efficiency Ratios	Forecast Year Ended: 2015	Forecast Year Ended: 2016
Net Profit / (Loss) Ratio Calculated as: • Net Profit Before Tax divided by Total Income	7.0%	14.7%
Sales and Service Income to Total Income Calculated as: • Total Sales and Service Income divided by Total Income • Sales and Service Income is income derived directly from core business training activities	100%	100%
Net Profit to Net Tangible Assets Calculated as: • Net Profit Before Tax divided by [Total Assets minus Intangible Assets minus Total Liabilities]	20.54%	36.46%

The Sections:
The Market

9

Your business operates in a competitive, survival-of-the-fittest environment that has no mercy. Besides you and your immediate sphere, very few people have any interest in whether you grow or even survive. So you need to do your homework and understand the jungle your business will live in. Knowing your market is crucial to enable you to

- Maintain a competitive advantage
- Develop your core messages, advertising, and tagline
- Target your marketing
- Reduce marketing costs
- Respond quickly and effectively to market changes
- Keep up with technology
- Maximize the chances of success
- Maximize profitability
- Identify opportunities and threats
- Get first move advantage for innovation

All sections under *The Market* are mandatory for all business plans. For *Plans for Yourself*, even if you have conducted market research a year earlier, it is prudent to regularly update your knowledge, as the market can change quickly, often without you realising. In *Plans for Others*, the reader and approver will want to know your business environment with great interest, as it will inform them of the opportunity, risk, and your readiness to deal with the challenges.

For a small business, there are limitations to how far you can go with market research, since you likely don't have the budget to buy high-level industry reports, conduct detailed surveys, or employ a team to research for you. As is customary for small business, you will have to roll up your sleeves and do it yourself, which in reality is more useful, since you will educate yourself along the way. It is important to keep perspective on the level of detail that you need to start or run your business better, which can be less in-depth. That is also the level that is appropriate for small business plans.

Common problems I see with this section include,

- It is omitted.
- Only headline numbers are included.
- The preferences and needs of the target market are not included.
- It is assumed that there is only one target market.
- The target market is "everyone."
- Competitors are not investigated.
- Information is not based on actual data with references.
- There is no attempt to interpret data to assist the business in developing a marketing strategy.
- Key messages are not developed or implemented.

Interpretation and Implications

As you go through each of the following sections, you must draw conclusions from each about where your business fits into the market, and position your business to give the greatest chance of success. Creating your value proposition must be done in the context of your market. If you can get your pricing right, marketing messages potent and well directed, value high, and customer experience rave-worthy, you are way ahead of the competition. The final result should be a compelling value proposition that sets you apart from your competitors or puts you in a new market. Quite often I hear small businesses talk about their "point of difference." Being different is only of value if it satisfies a need in your target market. After all, "different" could mean "better" or "worse."

Target Markets

Your target markets should be presented in your business plan in a simple, easy to understand way. Identify your top two to four markets, the products/services they will buy and then list their characteristics and wants as clients.

If you are currently in business, you will already know who your main client groups are, even if you have never defined them. They will buy in the same way or will have similar characteristics. For a new business, speak to other business owners, consultants or potential clients. Do some reading, and look at what your competitors are doing. It can be a good idea to get professional help if you are stuck on this. In *Plans for Yourself*, this section does not need to be completed in your initial plan, and it is suitable to be included as an action.

Typical classifications of your target market could include

- Individuals/businesses/governments/organisations
- Wholesale/retail
- Online/bricks and mortar

- Business size
- Geographic location
- Size of orders or purchases
- Type of business or organisation, such as schools, food, logistics, health
- Characteristics of individual clients, such as age, gender
- Interests of individual clients, such as golf, dogs, baking, books

What to Do

1. Create a table that lists your top two to four target markets.
2. For each market, list the characteristics you used above to define your markets. The more specific, the better value it is for you.
3. For each market, list their wants as buyers.

Example: Mortgage Broker

Market 1: First-home buyer
Market 2: Existing homeowner/upgrading/refinancing
Market 3: Investor

Market 1: First-home buyer
Description
- *Mid-20s*
- *Single or couple, generally without children*
- *Income 40K+*
- *Areas: inner city*
- *Ideal purchase $500K+*
- *Priorities—lifestyle*
- *Assets mostly furniture/cars*
- *Usually buying apartments*

Needs
- *Come with expectations—need to work out solution*
- *Need hand holding*
- *End-to-end guidance*

Messages
- *Focus on empowerment/enabling*
- *Support*
- *Facilitate process*
- *Expertise important*
- *Fresh, young professional image*

Actions
- *Leverage social networks*
- *Marketing focus on word of mouth*
- *Commonly all friends are buying*
- *Marketing messages*
- *Generally have no idea about process, so need complete guidance*

Example: Business Consultancy

All target markets are small businesses and defined by their current needs.

Market 1: Operating small businesses
Market 2: Start-up businesses
Market 3: Businesses applying for financing or loans

Description
- *Operating businesses three years or more*
- *Revenue $300,000 to $4M*
- *Queensland Australia*

Needs
- *Accurate*
- *Fast*
- *Cost effective*
- *Expertise*
- *Able to build strong relationships quickly*
- *Understand personalities*
- *Work within resource limitations*

Messages
- *Experienced and insightful*
- *Broad knowledge across all industries*
- *Good network of experts*
- *Understand small business*
- *Fairly priced*
- *Fast turnaround*

Market Size

Including an estimation of your market size can be a useful and interesting addition to your business plan, because it gives you a place in the scale of your industry and helps to crystallize longer-term goals. For small businesses, actually getting the data that will enable you to do the calculations can often be a roadblock, but give it a go to see how far you get.

For *Plans for Yourself*, this section does not need to be completed in your initial plan and is suitable to be included as an Action. For *Plans for Others*, only include it if you have completed the calculations and are confident of accuracy, or if the application requested this information.

What to Do

1. Start with each target market, and try to find available information for that market. In many cases, you will not find the exact number you are looking for, so you may need to do some estimations. The aim is to get an estimate of the number in that target market.

Example: Real estate agency services

- *Real-estate agents in Victoria. Look online or professional associations for an estimate.*
- *Girls in Brisbane between thirteen and eighteen. Australian Bureau of Statistics has population statistics, which should provide some data close to this.*
- *Schools in southern Sydney. Check the education department, or you may be able to purchase a list of schools you can then categorize yourself.*
- *Aged-care facilities. Can be found on an online guide.*

---

2. Estimate an average of how much you are likely to sell each member of that target market.

> *You intend to a new product to real estate agents in Victoria. There are two variations of the product, which you sell at $50 (25 percent of sales) and $100 (75 percent), so the average is $87.50. On average, you sell fifty products/ agency/year. Total value/agency =$4,375.*

3. Estimate the total. Calculate the total value of the market.

> *2,600 agencies in Victoria @ $4,375/agency =$11.375M*

What to Put in Your Plan

Make a brief statement of total estimated market value and your target for market penetration (which needs to be consistent with your projections). Put your assumptions in the Appendix.

Example: Property Business

> *<Business Name> estimates that the total market value for Real Estate Agencies in Victoria is $11.375M.*
> *The market penetration goal is 10 percent by December 31 2020, with sales of $1.14M. Assumptions are detailed in Appendix x.*

Market Trends

Business conditions are constantly changing from a local level to global. Changes as wide as local council regulations, technology, market preferences and fashion to global currency exchanges can all affect your business. Being aware of changes on the horizon is vital to successful business planning, as your planning will need to address these potential challenges.

For a small business, finding out what could potentially affect your business—with such a wide scope of events—is a daunting task, and it is not realistic to spend a huge amount of time or money to do so. That said, your business is a significant investment and risk to your financial health, so you need to do the best you can. It is wise to build these activities into your ongoing business management.

What to Do

1. Finding pertinent information can be time consuming, so knowledgeable people would be the best place to start:
    *   Speak to contacts in your industry, your service providers, or "switched-on" professionals in your sphere who work in accounting, legal, finance, or the stock market, as they often keep an eye on trends.
    *   Speak to similar, noncompeting businesses.

2. Do some research; the following sources are a good start.
    *   Industry journals, newspapers, and TV shows
    *   Bloggers and columnists who keep an eye on current events
    *   Business breakfasts
    *   Government and council sites
    *   Good business consultant

What to Put in Your Plan

Include a short statement about the changes happening in your market. Often you will discover changes that require action, which you can list in the same section, but it would be more common to list risks, SWOT, or as tasks in the relevant section(s).

Example: "Green" Building Products

- *Polyurethane products are still currently available in Australia but are not widely used in other parts of the world. Market activity internationally focused on natural products. There is no current legislation to change regulations, but such changes would significantly benefit <Business Name.>*
- *In Australia there is a growing demand for green products, with consumers becoming increasingly aware of environmental impact. Health issues caused by environmental factors and the provision of information about toxicity are also increasing. This growth will create an advantageous trading environment for <Business Name>.*

Example: Technology Company

The development industry is in its infancy, so there will be many changes as it becomes established. All these changes create enhanced business conditions for <Business Name>.

- *The market for developers to start and grow businesses is still wide open, so there is a window of opportunity to established a strong brand and capitalize on unmet demand. Competitors will move into the market, and undoubtedly, it will become crowded over time.*
- *Currently, 25 percent of development is outward facing for marketing and customer service applications. Future growth is expected to be dominated by internal development for business applications, rising to 80 percent in the future.*
- *Software development is in a migratory phase from desktop domination to mobile devices. Total spent on mobile is predicted to surpass desktop in the near future.*

Competition

Taking a good hard look at your competitors is essential to understanding where your business fits into the competitive landscape. You will discover things they do well and some they do poorly. Take a step outside your business to see where you fit, and more important, what your competitive advantage is. Ideally, this exercise re-enforces the differentiation that you already feel that you have.

What to Do

1. Start by creating a list of eight to fifteen competitors, including,
    *   Direct competitors (who offer essentially the same services)
    *   Indirect competitors, those who offer alternative services your clients may purchase instead of yours.

For example, a pole-dancing school looked at other pole-dancing studios as their direct competitors, but their indirect competitors included exercise classes, dance classes, and gyms.

2. Determine categories for comparison. Following is a sample a list of categories that might be useful for your analysis. Clearly, there are huge variations between businesses and industries, so go through the list and select those that are relevant to you, adding others you think are relevant.

Category	Explanation
Organisation name	Their business name
Products/services	Describe exactly what they sell and how it overlaps with your business.
Organisation/business type	For example, franchise, private company, public company, not-for-profit, family business
Tagline/USP	Do they have one? What is it? Is it memorable?
Address/location(s)/numbers of locations	For example, fifty offices throughout Victoria, headquarters in Sydney, Web business based in Brisbane
URL	www.theirdomainname.com.au (for later reference)
Target markets	Who are they selling to?
Contact details	If you feel that you want to contact them again later, this will save you time.

Years of operation	If you can find out, indicates longevity.
Areas serviced	For example, worldwide, local, Adelaide-only, remote services
Clients	Who do they service? Types of clients, companies, or note? Same target market as you?
Corporate image—comments	Colours inconsistent with target market? Good logo? Terrible tagline?
Website	Spend some time on their site. Get a feel for what they offer and how the site works, including navigation, design, message, effectiveness as marketing tool.
Price range	For example, medium, $50-$120, cheap
Industries/products that they specialize in	For example, plastics, aviation, engineering services to government
Industry standing/reputation	Look for media, PR, news, or similar
Customer value proposition—promoted	What are they saying is the reason you should do business with them?
Customer value proposition—perceived	Why do you think you should do business with them?
Other comments	Anything else of note that you discovered during your research

3. Set up a standard table to use for each competitor.

4. Conduct research. Use whatever means you are comfortable with to find out the information, including company websites, media, brochures, their clients, or pretending to be a customer. As you go, fill the information into the standard table to maintain consistency and not forget any details.

ORGANISATION	Business Name
Tagline / USP	Nice tagline
Web	www.businessname.com
Years of operation	More than 20 years.
Types of products / services	Software design & delivery, **tools, training, consulting**
Business size	Business name has grown from that small group in Chicago to a company of over 2500 passionate people spread across 29 offices in 12 countries: Australia, Brazil, Canada, China, Ecuador, Germany, India, Singapore, South Africa, Uganda, the United Kingdom, and the United States.
Comment of corporate image	Seems very progressive. Design fun but philosophical.
Target market	Large corporate. Clients listed include. NHS, Heart Foundation, BNB Co. Lots of American businesses.
Perceived differences from competitor	Promote as though leaders with software application, more that software or specific applications. Branding includes software development but position around approach and innovative problem solving.

Comments	Website it much less clear from homepage on what services are on offer.
	   · Messages around thinking are not clear.
	   · Broader than just apps, but doesn't really specify.
	   · Very big business, very capable, broad offering but maybe harder to identify for first time visitor.
	   · Lot more focus on platforms.
	   · Not much in case studies or examples.
	   · Website is much more philosophical

In your conclusion, make comparisons about how well each competitor does in the key categories. More importantly, you need to determine how you compare and where you fit into the market. The exact style will vary, depending on your own style and business, but core messages and differentiation need to be identified.

Example: Art Gallery/Cafe

Art spaces/galleries may be categorized based on ownership and objectives.

Not-for-profit. *Operated by councils or larger nonprofit organisations that exist to display artwork, foster development in the arts community, and generally do not sell artwork. On the peninsula, Gallery 1 and Peninsula Regional Gallery fall into this category.*

This category is indirect competition for <Business Name>, as it attracts art-loving patrons to alternative sites. Since purchase of artwork is generally not available, it is not direct competition. Through the fostering of interest in the arts, these galleries will indirectly contribute to the success of <Business Name>.

Commercial galleries. *Private businesses that operate display spaces with the intention of selling artworks. There are a number of galleries on the peninsula in this category, which vary in size, success, and type of art. This category is direct competition for <Business Name>.*

> *Currently, there are a small number of larger, successful commercial galleries that have operated and built their reputations over many years. There are fewer smaller commercial galleries of varying degrees of quality. Some have become rundown and appear neglected.*
>
> *We conclude that there are no art spaces that possess the exact attributes proposed by <Business Name>.*

Example: Recruitment Business

> *The recruitment industry has a large number of agencies, especially boutique agencies, that generally specialize in particular roles or industries. Even so, the exact roles and types of businesses each agency specializes in varies from agency to agency, even within the same industry.*
>
> *The client base (hence the types of roles) are often tied to the relationships established between the consultant and the client. The competitors investigated operate in the same space as <Business Name>, with varying degrees of overlap and breadth. Recruitment agencies within the industries of interest to <Business Name> are highly fragmented, with different agencies operating across a smaller subsection.*
>
> *The abilities already identified in <Business Name>, coupled with established relationships, are identified as key differentiators from competitors.*

Example: Online Homewares Business

> *Market positioning and branding of competitors varies enormously, starting from very kiddie, selling exclusively to children, and ranging up to stylish, up-market adult interiors. Most businesses have created branding and products targeted to their specific market. Few offer a broad range of products. There is very little customization in product design, with most businesses offering similar products.*
>
> *Most competitors sell predominantly through online stores, where the customer experience could be improved. In general, delivery information is hard to find until checkout is reached. The best sites have easy, clear navigation, product categories, advertise prices early on, and have clean design.*

> *<Business name> has created a higher-value customer proposition by offering a wider range of designs, price in mid-range, better colour ranges, customization more than all competitors, and designer product range. Our branding appeals to all categories. Our approach is sophisticated, with designs that appeal specifically to each sector.*

Technology

Changes in technology will have a big impact on the operation and profitability of your business, so it is important to know about changes and developments. This section will be brief and state what technological changes are currently in use, already on the market but not used, new developments, and what strategy or actions will be taken. For new businesses, state what types of technology will be in place when you start and any further implementations required in the short to medium term. This section could be included as an action in *Plans for Yourself* but is mandatory in *Plans for Others*.

Considerations could include,

- Software, such as accounting, operations
- Cloud, server, or mobile applications
- Developments in marketing
- Social media

What to Do

To find out what is on the horizon for your industry,

- Take some time to read industry journals, newspapers, and blogs.
- Speak to service providers that specialize in particular industries, such as your accountant or IT provider, as they will know what is happening in their industries.
- Speak to contacts in your industry.

Examples

Technology

Accounting

<Business Name> currently utilises MYOB V.x, located on the company server. Advances in cloud-based accounting software suggest that this may be an efficient replacement in the next twelve months. A research project will be conducted to assess viability, costs, and efficiencies.

Action: Review cloud-based accounting to determine whether it is suitable to replace current software.

Computers

Currently, <Business Name> utilises a xxx server located in our main office. A recent review has concluded that this will need replacement in the next six months.

Action: Review current IT needs, and assess need for upgrade of current equipment.

Operations Software

Research indicates that a new cloud-based booking system will improve efficiency and make customer payments and bookings significantly easier than the current Excel-based system. This system will be commissioned from January to March, with trials conducted April-June and full implementation in the new financial year in July.

10

The Sections:
Marketing and Sales

Marketing and sales is a very big topic, so planning for these activities could create a large document in its own right. In general, this section in business plans tends to be more of a summary. In this chapter, I describe the sales and marketing content required for business planning, not a full description of marketing plan development.

Common problems I see with this section include,

- The section looks too basic, as if it has been included as an afterthought.
- Marketing initiatives have not been well researched.
- Ideas and plans presented don't seem appropriate for the business.
- Budgets look like guesswork.
- Overall presentation makes marketing appear as afterthought.
- Essential marketing activities are left out.
- Marketing activities are not directly linked to the market research conducted in the "Market" section.

Plans for Yourself vs. Plans for Others

In *Plans for Yourself*, you will need enough detail to use it as a blueprint for your marketing activities, meaning you will list what you intend to do, when you intend to do it, and how much it will cost. It is common to have a list of actions as part of this, but they need times attached to ensure they are followed.

In *Plans for Others*, marketing and sales content is provided to round out your plan, show your proposal is solid, and you have thought out this aspect of your business. Not a great deal of detail is required, just an overview.

Marketing

The following structure is typical of a marketing section in a business plan, each of which is described in the sections that follow.

- Marketing overview
- Marketing materials
- Marketing initiatives

Marketing Overview

This section summarizes on a higher level the overall objectives of your marketing, what channels you intend to employ, broad objectives, and intended approach. The easiest way to create the summary is to do it when you have finished this chapter, so you can more easily summarize. This section needs to be completed in your plan and is not suitable to be included as an action.

Example: Cafe

> *No marketing is currently conducted by <Business Name>, with business growth only sustained through location, reputation, and word of mouth. During 2014, a program of sustained and ongoing marketing will commence in order to drive business growth.*
> *<Business Name> marketing aims to*
> - *Increase local contacts and profile*
> - *Increase all business, with new business especially focusing on catering and birthday cakes*
> - *Establish an Internet presence through a new website and social media campaigns*

Example: Allied Health Business

> *Marketing activities will focus on referrals from health professionals, so the <Business Name> marketing strategy will focus on*
> - *Brand development directly to health professionals*
> - *Educating health professionals about <Business Name> services*
> - *Motivating health professional to refer patients to <Business Name>*
> - *Establishing sales channels where health professional may on-sell <Business Name> services.*

Marketing Materials

This section describes the marketing materials you have or intend to develop. The level of detail will depend on your plan but will be very short in *Plans for Others*, or even omitted. Your description of marketing materials would include a list with brief summary. If you have examples that might be included, put them in the Appendix. In *Plans for Yourself*, it is quite common to identify that you need to create marketing materials when you are in the planning process and will create them during the period of implementation. This section does not need to be completed in your initial plan (unless specified) and is suitable to be included as an action.

Example: Building Company

Suggested Marketing Materials	For Use in
Folio of previous projects and company profile	Sales presentation
Promotional flyers (Good Neighbour Program)	Good neighbour program
Company brochures	Sponsorship, trade shows, direct mail, open house, sales presentations
Direct mail, meetings, and invitations to open houses	Strategic alliance
Invitations	Events: "Open house"
Signage	On-site display
Advertisement design (as required)	Advertising

> *Actions*
> - *Design and print company brochures*
> - *Review logo*

Marketing Initiatives

This section is the meatiest part of marketing and sales, where you summarize all the marketing initiatives you intend to undertake. *Plans for Yourself* and *Plans for Others* only differ in the level of detail.

What to Do

The easiest way to add a summary of marketing initiatives is to start with a master list, since it will include many initiatives; some of these you will not be aware of.

It sounds almost trivial to just create a list of initiatives to include in your business plan, but you will still spend time researching costs, times, publications, and other details of the initiatives that you choose. Comprehensive marketing research must be completed for all businesses, and no money should be spent until it is completed.

Plans for Others

The aim for including marketing initiatives in *Plans for Others* is to demonstrate that your business proposal is well formulated and rounded. Details are generally not required, so include a tabulated summary, including title and short description.

What to Do

1. Download a master list of initiatives from www. businessplancompany.com.au.
2. Add it to your plan.
3. Delete those initiatives that are not relevant to your business.
4. Edit each initiative so the descriptions exactly match your business needs.

Example: Consulting Business

Advertising	Place advertisements in business magazines and online business news sites.
Direct Marketing	Telesales campaign to Sydney-based, medium-sized businesses
Sponsorship	Gold sponsor and business breakfast
Networking	Attendance and accountants society annual conference and monthly meeting
Social media	Ongoing regular communications on Facebook, Twitter, and Tumblr

Plans for Yourself

For *Plans for Yourself,* include more detail. How much depends on whether you are a new or operating business and how much time you have during your planning. This might include specifics of each initiative, such as costs, time frames, previous results, publications, or sponsorship opportunities. Everything you don't have time to do during planning will be listed as an action.

What to Do

1. Download a master list of initiatives from www.businessplancompany.com.au.
2. If you are in business already, compare the initiatives listed with your previous activities, assessing those that have been effective in your business and those that have not.
3. Add it to your plan.
4. Delete those initiatives that are not relevant to your business.
5. For each initiative. research costs and determine timing.
6. Add relevant detail and schedule into your plan.
7. Edit each initiative, so the descriptions exactly match your business needs.
8. Add details of your research, and create an action list.

Example: New Recruitment Business

Database
The sourcing, installation, and population of a client and candidate management database is high priority.
Description
The client database forms a foundation of marketing infrastructure, enabling the creation of a vital marketing resource that will impact the growth and development of all business units.

Value
- *Enables the development of a dedicated list of current and potential clients and candidates*
- *Facilitates ongoing communications for business information, relationship development and promotion*
- *Enables categorization of database, enabling rapid contact to promote or identify candidate communication of information relevant to their interest*
- *Regular communication*
- *Maintain <Business Name> "top of mind" in client base*
- *Inform target market about seasonal events, special offers, news, etc.*
- *Generate sales and other interactions*
- *Increase Web traffic*
- *Increase word-of-mouth activity and viral marketing*

Type of Communication or Materials
1. *Monthly communications to clients (e-news)*
   - *Candidates of interest*
   - *Industry news*
2. *Monthly communications to candidates (e-news)*
   - *Industry news*
   - *Referral programs or other special offers*
3. *Regularly scheduled phone contact with key contacts and clients*

Costs
Database costs estimate $2,750.
Ongoing salary cost for communications $1,200/month.

Actions
Source and install client management database.
Segment database and develop schedule for contact.

Marketing Schedule

Including a summary of your proposed marketing activities with costs and timing is a sound addition to your business planning, as it clarifies spending and timing. It gives you a snapshot of your marketing plan at a glance. This is a vital part of *Plans for Yourself* but would be rare in *Plans for Others*. It's a simple display of an annual schedule that lists the initiatives you are going to conduct with accurate estimates of how much each is going to cost and when it will be done. Total costs for each month and initiative should be calculated to create your annual budget.

As with determining marketing initiatives, this can take time, so it would be fine to include this as an action, but keep it a high priority, as it needs to be organized early.

What to Do

- In the schedule template (download from businessplancompany.com.au), add all marketing initiatives with months that money will be spent. Also add timing for free initiatives.
- Include a contingency amount for additional initiatives that may come up during the year that you think are worthwhile.

Example: Gift Shop/Online Store

In this table, activities are highlighted for the months they are planned, with costs—if any— in the same cell.

Activity	Comments	Jan	Feb	Mar	Apr	May	Jun	July	Aug	Sep	Oct	Nov	Dec	Totals
Seasonality considerations														
School terms returning														
Christmas														
End of financial year														
Advertising														
Industry magazines				$400.00	$500.00		$500.00		$500.00		$500.00		$500.00	$2,500.00
Industry association									$400.00					$800.00
Networking	Free monthly events for members													$ -
Direct marketing														
Schools campaign			$250.00	$250.00	$250.00	$250.00	$250.00	$250.00	$250.00	$250.00	$250.00	$250.00	$250.00	$2,500.00
PR														
PR submissions via website, monthly	Free			$200.00	$200.00	$200.00	$200.00	$250.00	$200.00	$200.00	$200.00	$200.00	$200.00	$2,000.00
Public speaking														$ -
Sponsorship														
Mother's group walk											$4,500.00			$4,500.00
Marketing materials														
Catalogues	8 individual brochures - in folder	$100.00		$1,500.00	$10,000.00		$2,000.00	$100.00	$2,000.00		$2,000.00		$2,000.00	$19,500.00
Promo products					$100.00						$100.00			$400.00
Photos					$1,500.00									$1,500.00
Pens			$560.00											$560.00
B Cards				$500.00										$500.00
Banners				$140.00										$140.00
Notepads				$200.00										$200.00
Trade shows														
Industry trade show	$2500 stand - $10000							$4,000.00	$3,000.00				$3,000.00	$10,000.00
Events														
In-house training events	$400 per event - every 2nd month					$300.00		$300.00		$300.00		$300.00		$1,200.00
Website														
	ongoing updates		$150.00					$150.00						$300.00
Internet Marketing														
Adwords		$250.00	$250.00	$1,000.00	$1,000.00	$1,000.00	$1,000.00	$1,000.00	$1,000.00	$1,000.00	$1,000.00	$1,000.00	$1,000.00	$10,000.00
Yellow Pages Online		$250.00	$250.00	$250.00	$250.00	$250.00	$250.00	$250.00	$250.00	$250.00	$250.00	$250.00	$250.00	$3,000.00
Business Development / Strategic Sales														
Telesales		$100.00	$100.00	$100.00	$100.00	$100.00	$100.00	$100.00	$100.00	$100.00	$100.00	$100.00	$100.00	$1,200.00
Contingency														
Additional unexpected campaigns		$500.00	$500.00	$500.00	$500.00	$500.00	$500.00	$500.00	$500.00	$500.00	$500.00	$500.00	$500.00	$6,000.00
		$950.00	$1,660.00	$5,040.00	$14,400.00	$2,690.00	$4,960.00	$6,850.00	$7,890.00	$3,000.00	$9,400.00	$2,600.00	$7,890.00	$65,800.00

Website

Your website is a core part of your business infrastructure, hence it needs some description in your business plans. In *Plans for Others*, the aim is to include two to three paragraphs that round out your proposal and make it appear well designed and valuable contributor to your business. However, if your website is a central part of your business model (like an online store or technology business), it should be described in much more detail.

In *Plans for Yourself*, the level of detail will depend on your stage of business. New businesses should describe detail about structure, design, and function for the purposes of doing the necessary research and development ahead of building the site. If you have an operating business, this section will describe changes, developments, or plans for the site. In both cases, it is acceptable to have future developments listed as actions, so long as they are completed before any developments take place.

For detailed sections, you may include detail such as,

- objectives for your site;
- key functionalities; for example, bookings, communications, quotes;
- how the site will be used by clients;
- how the site will be used by team members;
- marketing objectives;
- online store;
- interaction with social media; and
- mobile functionality.

Example: Technology Company (*Plan for Others*)

Website

Registered domain name: www.mybusinessname.com.au. A website is currently under development that will have the following sections.

- Home	- About Us
- Work	- Technologies (NodeJS [Sails], Appcelerator
- Contact	Titanium, Grails, Backbone.js,
- Blog	Responsive, Git)

Example: Coaching Company (*Plan for Yourself*)

Website

Content and Functions

- Provide information about <Business Name> services
- Find information about industry, regulations, general usage of products and services
- Get advice or information through direct person-to-person contact
- Join database
- Make bookings or reservations for events
- Obtain resources, articles, tools, etc.

Content and Pages

1. Marketing. Build credibility through
   - Logos of member organizations or professional associations: Australian APT, British Psychological Society, ICF, CFA
   - Qualifications
   - Case studies
   - Testimonials
   - Include blog or forum for discussion and/or advice on career transition and opportunity for participants to ask questions.
2. Company and service information
   - Give overview of programs, packages and outcomes
   - History, experience, benefits
3. Motivate to take action
   - Strong call to actions
   - Downloadable report, white paper, and mailing list subscription
4. Members area
   - Coaching resources to assist clients in the application of their programs both during the program and thereafter; e.g., skills/technique related information, links to useful sites and databases, networks, book references
   - Some downloadable information related to program implementation
   - Repository of working documents, such as exercises, tools

---

Sales

Sales is a broad topic with many elements that differ greatly across different businesses, including everything from point of sale to account management. In general, you wouldn't include this section for *Plans for Others* unless it is of particular interest to building your business case. For example, a financier for a new business might be interested in a summary of how you will secure sales.

In *Plans for Others*, this section should be included and developed to the highest level of detail that time permits. Everything else these should be actions. Again, these areas need to be developed to give you the best chance of success.

In this section you might include descriptions of any of the following sales processes and initiatives that are relevant to your business.

- *Sales process*—describe the process your business follows when making sales.
- *Telesales/direct sales*—describe strategies and processes for these types of sales campaigns.
- *Account management*—give details of how larger client accounts will be maintained and grown.
- *Promotions*—list ongoing, regular, or one-off sales promotions you will have during the year.
- *Online sales*—describe how you promote and foster online sales.
- *Point of sale*—list ways in-store marketing and promotion stimulate sales.
- *Quotes*—describe the quoting process and how you maximize outcome.
- *Retail*—list the strategies you use in store to generate sales.

- *Tenders, grants, and bids*—list those you will pursue and how you will do so.

Example: Professional Services Business

Sales

Sales Process

1. First contact

    - Telephone, e-mail, referral, or in person

2. Meeting

    - Attend meeting with prospective clients

    - Understand client needs

    - Explain services

    - Move towards becoming a client of AA

3. Proposal

    - Send all details of services with proposal

4. Follow up

    - Make contact to determine interest in services

5. Trial

    - If needed to reassure client, conduct trial services

6. Contract

    - Review contracts

    - Make changes as necessary

    - Sign contracts

Account Management

Account management will be an essential component of client retention in order to identify issues, maintain quality, and foster open communication. Senior management will need to:

    - Create a structured review schedule

    - Communicate regularly with REA management by telephone and in person

    - Act swiftly on any feedback that requires action

Actions

    - Create sales tracking system

    - Account management

    - Folio for promotion

11

The Sections: Operations

The "Operations" section describes how your business will operate. The intention is not to write a policies and procedures manual here but to give an overview and highlight main business functions. Imagine that you are explaining how your business operates to someone who knows nothing about it. That's what this section is for. Again, the level of detail will be dictated to by the purpose of your plan and the stage of your business.

Plans for Others will briefly describe the key functions of your business at a higher level, so the reader gets a good, broad overview of how your business functions and reinforces your organisation and forward thinking. Go into more detail for those sections that are important to the functioning of the business and those aspects that may be new, novel, or complex.

Plans for Yourself for operating businesses should include changes to your operations, measures of current operations, and goals for your operations within the time frame of the plan or reviews of operations. It would be quite common to include such issues as actions.

Plans for Yourself for new businesses should go into as much detail as you have time to do. This exercise is excellent for uncovering lots of hidden issues that you had not thought of before, so it can alert you to all sorts of dangers as well as truly clarify what you will do. It forces you to get actual data on how things work.

In the rest of this chapter you will find sections that may or may not apply to your business. Choose only to add those relevant to your business.

Common problems I see with this section include,

- Sections are included with incorrect level of detail—too much or too little.
- It is not included at all, is too basic or very brief.
- New businesses tend to add only information they know without much research.
- Most important functions are not highlighted.

Operations—Overview and Business Process

The reader already knows you sell socks, repair cars, design buildings, and so on. But he or she won't know the steps involved in how you make that happen. This section gives an overview of it all, with some more detail in later sections. The information in this section can be presented in many ways and will vary a lot in length, depending on your business and who will read your plan. In the following examples, several examples are given and types of businesses for which they might be applicable. This section needs to be completed in your initial plan and is not suitable to be included as an action.

Example: Carwash

Operational Plan

The four brothers who will be directors of <Business Name> will be responsible for all operational management. Since the carwash is automated, it is anticipated that the time commitment per day will be approximately two hours. Additional after-hours emergency management and customer support will be provided on a rotational basis.

Activities will include
- Emptying
- Cleaning
- Refilling
- General maintenance
- Emptying

Security

The following security measures will be employed.
- Twenty cameras relaying live surveillance to the office via the Internet
- Security alarm system
- Metal doors with protective gates after hours
- All vending machines enclosed with security features

Customer Support

A contact telephone number with direct access to the owners will be provided, so customers may contact management directly in the event of an emergency or requiring customer support.

Example: Small Manufacturer

3.1 Production

Currently products are completely assembled by *<Business Name>*, as shown below.

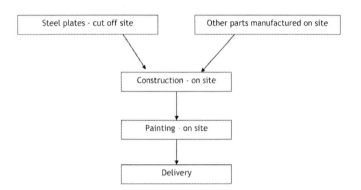

Utilising current production processes, it is expected that production capacity will be 15-20 units per week. As the volume of orders grows, a greater number of 'on-site' parts manufacture will be sent off-site for manufacture.

Due to the fact that the business will be operated as a sole trader, attention will be paid to managing time across manufacturing, sales, marketing, accounts, etc.

Current infrastructure will meet the business requirements for the medium term.

Inventory, Sourcing, and Logistics

For those businesses that manufacture, import, export, move, store, or sell products, inventory management, sourcing, and logistics are crucial to efficiency, cash flow, and profitability. Business planning around these issues is focused on understanding them, knowing how they will affect your business, and identifying opportunities to improve.

These business functions are usually complex, and doing extensive reviews of movements, suppliers, and costs may be limited by time. If you are writing a plan for others, this would typically be a summary section that explains the most important details unless it is central to your business. In *Plans for Yourself*, the level of detail you include will depend on the amount of time you have available. However, it is common to include actions for more thorough reviews later.

If you are starting a new business, you may still be sourcing suppliers and working out costing fundamentals essential to understanding your pricing and profitability. Make sure these fundamental issues are sorted before you start trade. During the research stage, you may do such activities as

- Source new suppliers.
- Compare prices, specifications, and quality of products.
- Research and compare freight and courier costs.
- Calculate turnover cycles and order and delivery times.
- Determine acceptable inventory levels and their effects on cash flow.
- Review security and exclusivity of supply agreements.
- Research alternative storage arrangements.
- Storage
- Payment cycles

Example: Chemical Company

Inventory Management	
Storage	Current storage in Melbourne (Boronia) is adequate for 1000-2000L. Queensland storage space is yet to be determined.
Payments	30 percent on delivery 40 percent at thirty days 30 percent at sixty days
Turnover cycles per year	Current product issues have prevented ordering of more than minimum stock orders. Now that product issues have been solved, order periods will be extended to eight to thirteen weeks.
Delivery times for customer needs; lead times for inventory resupply	From time of purchase order: Manufacture two weeks Transport four to six weeks

Action
- Develop inventory and supply management system.

Equipment, IT, and Infrastructure

Equipment and infrastructure will be included in those business plans where there is a change in the current situation or a need for change, particularly for new and growing businesses. In this section you briefly highlight the needs of the business for the planning period.

In *Plans for Others*, this section will be brief, such as a table or list that indicates the most important elements that will help to build your case. In some cases, your business will rely on specific or custom equipment that may need further detail, with costs included in this section or in "The Numbers." As always, if particular equipment is vital to your business or it is new or novel, go into more detail to give the reader clarity.

Plans for Yourself will include details of significant equipment, needs, or changes. If your business is starting, that will mean listing significant equipment to ensure you fully understand what you will need and the associated costs. Detailed costings will also be included in start-up costs. If your business is operating, your planning should include any challenges you are having with your current equipment and any plans for new equipment. Quite often these will be listed as actions to be addressed later. For example, if your production equipment is ageing, you may conduct a project to investigate upgrade options.

Typical inclusions for this section would be

- Manufacturing equipment
- Storage equipment
- Factory
- IT equipment
- Vehicles

Example: Hardware-Importing Business

Equipment and Infrastructure
Factory and production

Current factory and equipment are working well for current trade, with capacity to increase by 25 percent which, under current growth projections, will exceed capacity by December. <Business Name> has identified the following items that will need upgrade and expansion in the new calendar year to facilitate growth.
- *Drum handling equipment*
- *Decanting equipment*
- *Small forklift*
- *Rack storage*

Action: *Source suppliers and prices for new equipment.*

IT

Current IT infrastructure is not adequate to meet current company needs, with new systems already sourced and ready for implementation. The new systems will have capabilities and interactivity in the following areas.

- *Customer relationship management*
- *Accounting*
- *Logistics management*
- *Sales management*
- *Costs management*
- *Training*
- *Support*
- *Remote access*

Vehicles

Current vehicles are sufficient for company needs for the projected twelve-month growth.

Example: Contracted Services Business

<Business Name> will utilize two systems to communicate internally and with clients.

- *softwarename.com.au is industry software that will be used to collect attendee details, ideally linked back to clients who can access data directly.*
- *Rostering software (e.g., Deputy) will be linked directly to accounting software (e.g., Xero) in order to*
- *Create schedules*
- *Approve schedules*
- *Transfer data for invoicing*
- *Transfer data for payroll*

Actions

Internal IT: Finalize selection and set up.	*High*
REA IT: Create process to tap into REA clients' software.	*Medium*

Human Resources (HR)

If you are a sole trader, employees will not a have role in your business. At the opposite end, a larger service business is totally reliant on its team to exist. With such a wide spectrum of HR planning possible, your activities could sit anywhere, and the amount of time spent, attention given, and space in your plans will correlate. Given the amount that you could potentially include in this section, finding the right balance will start with being clear in your objectives.

If you are creating a plan for others, keep it concise and relevant to your application. Focus on the content that will help you. In many cases, this section is more about building the overall picture that you have a well-planned business in front of you rather than giving volumes of information.

If you are creating a *Plan for Yourself*, keep focused on the issues requiring current attention. In an operating business, use this opportunity to review current functioning, identifying issues and creating a plan of action. These are mostly added as actions to be implemented later.

If your business is starting, the purpose is to identify the most important issues and tasks needed to build your team with good systems, strong culture, and compliance with employment law. For new businesses, go as far as you need to be able to competently get started, with actions to implement as you trade. For example, having an organisational chart is an essential component, whereas developing a professional development program is less urgent.

If you don't have any staff, make a simple statement that explains this, such as "<Business Name> will be operated for this period as a sole trader without employees."

What to Include

In the following table, I have listed many subsections that could be included, with a guide of when they are relevant.

Section	Plans for Others	Plans for Yourself	Comments
Team/ organisational chart	Yes	Yes	
Roles and responsibilities	Yes	Yes[1]	• A short summary for each role helps explain the organisational chart. • In some applications, further detail will be mandated. • Include CV' of people taking on key roles if needed. [1]If job descriptions are not active, include as actions.
Recruitment	No[2]	Maybe[3]	[2]Unless it plays an important role in your business. [3]List as actions where development is needed.
Internal communication	No[2]	Maybe[3]	[2]Unless it plays an important role in your business. [3]List as actions where development is needed.
Induction and training	No[2]	Maybe[3]	[2]Unless it plays an important role in your business. [3]List as actions where development is needed.
Performance measurement	No[2]	Maybe[3]	[2]Unless it plays an important role in your business. [3]List as actions where development is needed.
Professional development	No[2]	Maybe[3]	[2]Unless it plays an important role in your business. [3]List as actions where development is needed.

Staff motivation and reward	Nº2	Maybe[3]	[2]Unless it plays an important role in your business. [3]List as actions where development is needed.

Example: Roles and Responsibilities—Health Business

Team

The <Business Name> operations team at the first studio will consist of

Managing Director—Name 1. Please find CV in appendix 7.1.

Office Manager/Administrator. Full time. Experienced medical/practice/office manager with strong attention to detail, capability to build business systems and oversee seamless service.

Receptionist/Administrator. Casual, to work additional hours, after hours, and Saturdays.

Bookkeeper. Under contract at commencement, moving to employee as the business grows.

Senior Motion Analyst. Full time. Likely to be a physiotherapist, exercise physiologist, or suitably qualified professional with high-level customer-service skills, a love of technology, and solid grounding in human movement.

Junior Motion Analyst. Casual, multiple positions to work additional and after hours, depending on demand. Likely to be physical sciences student or similar.

Business Consultant. Contract as needed. Business set up and growth specialist to advise on all aspects of business operations, strategy, and marketing.

Example: Roles and Responsibilities—Bakery Being Taken over by Staff

The <Business Name> team will remain unchanged, except for a small reduction in casual front of house hours.	
Kitchen	Head Chef—Michelle, thirty-two hours/week 2nd Chef—Mia, forty hours/week Chef—Daniel, forty hours/week
Front of House	Owner 1, fifty hours/week Owner 2, fifty hours/week

Management
- Owner 1 manages front and kitchen in the mornings.
- Owner 2 manages front and kitchen in the afternoon.

Occupational Health and Safety

Occupational health and safety is a complex area and needs expert involvement in your business. Including details of your policies and systems is not required, and a short summary will be adequate. If you are creating a *Plan for Others*, assure your reader that you are compliant with a short statement of the systems you are using. In *Plans for Yourself*, simply identify current needs and any actions that need to be taken.

Risks

Risk assessments in small business are pretty much unheard of, but a basic assessment of risks is an easy activity that can be useful to the business owner and show a reader that you have thought through your proposal. The easiest way to do this exercise is to put together a list of risks and then accompany each with simple strategies for how you might mitigate them. When you are in the creation process, ask a diverse group of people for feedback, particularly people who tend to be negative or suspicious. There is a generic list of typical risks available for download at www.businessplancompany.com.au that can help prompt your ideas. This section should be completed in your initial plan.

Examples: Risks I Have Seen in Small Business Plans

Risk	Strategy to Minimize
Revenue targets not met	Cash flow from existing business can be utilized until such time that sufficient cash flow is generated. Maintain consistent marketing activity.
Fallout in relationships between directors	Agreements will specify mechanism and conditions for one or more shareholders to leave. Sufficient levels of capital (or access to) will be kept within the family to enable buyout is required.
Competitors opening up nearby	Maintain high level of customer service and support. Continually upgrade and improve products and facilities to ensure clients have newest and best available. Maintain current facilities so is the most attractive. Already outperforming competitors in current business.
Equipment failure	Equipment has warranty with service, twenty-four-hour call out. Maintenance contract once initial warranty expires
Sabotage/vandalism	Security (see Section 8.2).
Fire or other destructive event	Insurance that covers all potential events, protection of income, etc. Loss of income, comprehensive.
Damage to cars through misuse	Insurance.

Automatic machines scratch or damage cars	*Insurance.*
Chemical reaction to paint	*Treat through polish.* *Absorb cost (this is low cost).*
Economic climate deteriorating or lasting for extended period of time, thus reducing budgets and/or delaying project start dates.	*Maintain very active and persistent sales and marketing activities.* *Constantly review market conditions to assess business activities, and adjust as required.* *Develop effective financial management systems.*
Incapacitation or death of either partner	*Develop plans for backup.* *Document systems, processes, and policies.* *Ensure all business processes are well measured.* *Ensure knowledge of other areas of business is sufficient to manage.*
Illness of either partner	*As above.* *Maintain adequate insurance.*
Loss of data	*Maintain adequate backup systems.*
SharePoint not adopted by market	*Adopt another system.*
Problems with relationship of business partners	*Develop effective agreements for business ownership and management.* *Follow schedule for regular communications.*
Business not achieving targets	*Review business planning and strategy regularly.* *Maintain very active and persistent sales and marketing activities.*
MS may end up hosting applications.	*Move into bigger more customized environments.* *Watch movements at MS.* *Target bigger clients.*
Market saturation. Because the market is limited, only a specific number of products may be sold in each category.	*Develop export strategy.* *Further product development.*
Reliance on Gordon. *Time limitations* *Risk in physical capacity*	*Maintain adequate insurance.* *Maintain effective time management strategies.* *Plan production.* *Occupational health and safety*

Product liability	*Maintain adequate insurance.*
	Create operational instructions to be included with each item sold.
	Ensure legal advice is sought.

Timeline

Timelines and project plans are very useful for new businesses and those businesses where you are undergoing a larger change, such as setting up new premises. These will add depth and strength to *Plans for Others*, where an overview table/chart is appropriate. In *Plans for Yourself*, add more detail to make this a workable blueprint.

Example: New Studio Set Up

	Nov	Dec	Jan	Feb	Mar	Apr	May	Jun	Jul	Aug	Sep
Finalize business plan	▓										
Secure funding	▓	▓									
Find and secure premises		▓	▓	▓							
Premises fit out					▓	▓	▓				
Import and install equipment						▓	▓				
Marketing planning		▓	▓	▓							
Marketing activities					▓	▓	▓				
Recruit staff						▓	▓				

Train staff							▓	▓			
Set up IT systems							▓				
Trading								▓	▓	▓	▓

Other Sections

There will be other operational details of relevance and interest to particular industries and circumstances that you may want to include or that a particular application may require. As always, keep the content succinct and relevant.

Examples of additional sections include,

- Security
- Customer service
- Technical support
- Quality control
- Opening hours
- Resources
- Intellectual property

12

The Sections: Action Plan

The action plan is where your business planning takes a leap off your page and becomes a priority list you implement in your business. Actions and the action plan are only included in *Plans for Yourself*. The aim is to create a prioritized list of projects and initiatives you and your team will work on to grow your business.

What to Do

1. When creating your business plan, you will have added actions in many sections as you went along.
2. Once your business plan is finished, go through each section, and create a list of all actions with their priorities.
3. Order the list by priority.
4. Within each priority group, order all items by urgency. If you have a lot in the high-priority group, order those and then review the others later.
5. Assign a month the action needs to be completed.
6. Reorder by due date.

Example

June-August

Action	Priority	Who
Develop interview tools, job ads, and reference checks for agents.	High	Rob
Develop interview tools, job ads, and reference checks for salesperson.	High	Rob
Website	High	Dave
Define company values.	High	Jess
Develop directors' agreements.	High	Lawyer
Develop contractor and supply agreements.	High	Lawyer
Set up accounting software.	High	Elle
Set up rostering software with invoicing and payroll.	High	Elle
Take out insurances when first client is secured.	High	Jane

Later

Action	Priority	Who
Create marketing materials: brochure, business cards.	High-Medium	Rob
Create sales presentation folio.	High-Medium	Jane
Develop subcontractor agreements.	Medium	Lawyer
Finalize and set up internal IT.	Medium	Dex
Create HR policies.	Medium	Rob
Create systems for each new client to ensure processes and procedures suit needs of REA.	Medium	Jane

13

The Sections:
Additional Information

In this final section of your plan, you include any additional information and references the reader may want to investigate further. References and appendixes are mandatory in *Plans for Others*, as they may want to check your claims for validity. In *Plans for Yourself* keeping references is good practice but not mandatory, as it makes your life easier if you want to relocate the source.

References

When you make a direct reference to external information in your plan, you need to quote the source. This gives authority to your statement, enables the reader to check if needed, and prevents any form of plagiarism. In the body of your plan, include a superscript number at the point you make a statement and then give the reference against the same number in the reference section. For example, "populations is predicted to grow by 1.8%"[2]

When listing references, there are many strict academic systems that you can follow if you are familiar with them. Such formality is less important in a small-business plan, where the reader just wants to be able to find the source information if he or she wants to.

Include as much detail as you have for author, date, URL, title, page, and chapter. In many cases, you will be citing information you found on the Web. In that case, include the URL but also the other information, so the reader can find it later if the URL changes.

Example

1. May 6, 2014, "Trends in Household Debt," Australian Bureau of Statistics, "4102.0—Australian Social Trends, 2014." *www.abs.gov.au/ausstats/abs@.nsf/ Lookup/4102.0main+features202014#SUSTAINABILITY.*

Appendixes

In each appendix you will include grouped information that is a further resource to the reader and builds a stronger case around your statements in the business plan. This could include many types of information

- Quotes, costs, and prices that you have described in your plan
- Details of project cost projections
- Details of financial projections
- Official documents, leases, permits, and so on
- Licence, accreditation, or membership documents
- CV
- Academic records
- Examples of work
- Information about prototypes, and so on

- Diagrams and drawings

For each distinct information type, give that section and different appendix number.

Example

> *Appendix 1: Professional Accreditation Certificate*
> *Appendix 2: Details of Start-Up Costs*
> *Appendix 3: Floor Plans of Proposed Restaurant*
> *Appendix 4: Council Planning Permit for Restaurant*
> *Appendix 5: Food Handling Certificate*